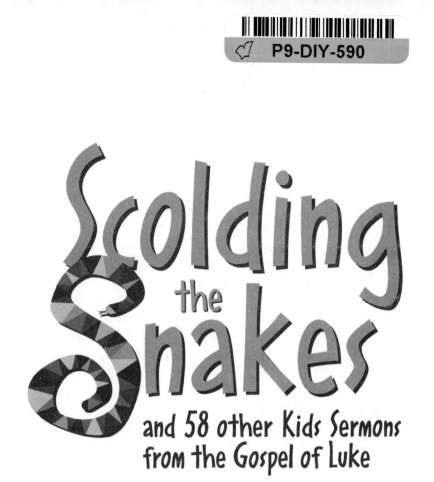

Scolding the Snakes

and 58 other Kids Sermons from the Gospel of Luke

Ruth Gilmore

Augsburg

MINNEAPOLIS

To Mom and Dad
with love

Cover design by Marti Naughton
Cover graphics by EyeWire
Book design by Michelle L. Norstad

Library of Congress Cataloging-in-Publication Data
Gilmore, Ruth, 1962-
  Scolding the snakes : and 58 other kids sermons from the Gospel of Luke / Ruth Gilmore.
    p. cm.
  Includes index.
  ISBN 0-8066-4082-0 (alk. paper)
  1. Children's sermons.
BV4315.G39 2000
252'.53—dc21   00-041624

The paper used in this publication meets the minimum requirements of American National Standard for Information Sciences—Permanence of Paper for Printed Library Materials, ANSI Z329.48-1984. ♾ ™

Manufactured in the U.S.A.   AF 9-4082

04   03   02   2   3   4   5   6   7   8   9   10

Contents—Series C

Sunday	Theme	Page

Scolding the Snakes

Foreword
by Walter Wangerin, Jr.

Ruth Gilmore has gathered together bright, brief patterns for communicating core truths of lessons in the Revised Common Lectionary.

As worship itself engages more than half our senses, so sound, sight, touch, motion, and discovery—and the near presence of the storyteller—all draw children, Sunday by Sunday, chapter by chapter, into the one real story of our salvation.

Here are little stories. Here are suggestions for tactile interaction. Here are frameworks for your own personal stories.

But the proclamation itself waits for you and for the dramatic moment when you engage the senses, the fierce interest, and the hearts of children.

Two things only will fill Gilmore's bright patterns with the power of a living Lord, and both things are called by the same name: love.

If you love the Lord of the story with your entire being, your telling will find its most persuasive style, *your* style, the manner you use when there is nothing more important to tell another soul than this. In you, the story will flare and live—and you, your presence and your person, will become the manifest evidence of it.

And if you love the children arrayed before you, you will design and tell that story specifically for *them*. You will watch them and be alert to their tiniest signs of attention. You will rejoice when the story goes home to their hearts, and they will see your joy, and their delight will grow even keener.

As Ruth Gilmore invites you to proclamation in these pieces, accept the invitation with love!

Introduction

"Let the little children come to me, and do not hinder them, for the kingdom of heaven belongs to such as these" (Matt. 19:14 NIV). Jesus' words remind us to see a child through the eyes of God—not as a noisy distraction from business at hand but as an honored inheritor of God's kingdom and a model of humility. Children, dancing their way through life, not yet filled with pride and self, still delightfully saturated with the joy of living—*they* embrace the kingdom. They live in the moment of grace.

This book offers fifty-nine chances to interact with children during worship services. Children's time is a magical moment in the church service. When young ones are invited forward, many will spring from their seats and gallop to the front of the church, thrilled to sit next to you and have the attention of the whole congregation. And the idea of hearing a good story told just for them, or the chance to unravel the meaning of an intriguing object lesson—well, these are opportunities just too good to pass up.

So, right from the start, all the advantages belong to you.

Stories have power.
Even as you capture the children's attention, adults in the congregation will be drawn into the story, hearing Bible truths told in a new way, appreciating the simplicity you bring to the message. We are—all of us—children, the sons and daughters of our heavenly Parent. Jesus reaches out to the child in each of us, teaching through stories and parables, because all children love a good story.

The sermons in this book ask you to be a storyteller. Each one is self-contained and ready to use. But before you begin, here are tips to sharpen your storytelling skills and make these children's sermons the most effective they can be.

Use sermons that work for you.
If you are following the Revised Common Lectionary, you will find that each sermon is based on one of the texts for the day. There are fifty-nine sermons in all, covering the entire church year, including special non-Sunday events and festivals. If you are not following a lectionary, you can search the contents list by theme or topic to find applicable sermons.

Build relationships.
Many sermons in this book make use of a personal anecdote or illustration. Children love to hear real-life stories about their elders, especially if they like the elders who are telling the stories. The relationship with your listeners has a lot to do with the connection you build in your first moments with them. It is important to be on their level—physically as well as intellectually. Sit with the children and recognize the importance of each child with your gestures and eye contact. Make it clear that you are eager to travel into the story with them.

And it's good to remember that our preconceived ideas about teaching and learning may be wrong. Even though we might really want our listeners to sit quietly and keep their eyes glued on us, some children learn best while in motion. Some of my most active listeners often turn out to be ones who most fully understand the point I am trying to make.

Keep it simple, brief, concrete.
I have tried to keep the language of these sermons simple and direct, easily understandable to children. Most sermons will take five minutes or less to deliver. Children's attention is a tenuous and precious thing. They are intent on soaking in every miracle of the world around them, and to concentrate on one thing at a time is a considerable challenge.

Many sermons make use of a simple object to illustrate a lesson. (A brief note at the beginning of each sermon will alert you to any special preparations or props.) Children will understand and retain more as more of their five senses are engaged. Their sense of touch or smell or taste will draw them back into the sermon and remind them of the truth that was taught. And with God's grace, they will learn that truth by heart.

Make the sermons your own—the CD ROM.

As was noted earlier, these sermons can be used just as they are—read directly from the page. *But they will be even better with a bit of preparation and personalization.* Use the enclosed CD to customize each sermon for the most appropriate delivery for your situation, for your audience. Add or substitute your own interesting, relevant stories wherever possible. Build in anecdotes, illustrations, and names from your congregation, city, or community.

Prepare.

It's always better to tell your sermon than to read it. The more familiar you are with the sermon, the easier it will be to *talk* to your listeners. In a well-rehearsed play, the trappings of the performance fade into the background while the emotion and meaning of the play come into focus. A performer who knows a part well is able to ad-lib if occasion demands.

And while you are sharing your sermons, don't be surprised if a kid puts his or her oar in. That may shift your direction slightly; but if you're prepared, you can go with the flow while continuing to steer gently. The bank you end up traveling to may be more interesting and important than the place you were originally headed.

Visit our Web site, too!

If you have a Web browser, you can find helpful information and resources about children's sermons at <**www.kid-sermons.com**>. There you'll be able to contact the author, read anecdotes, download scripts for puppet shows, find

information about other books in the series, and access links to other helpful sites on the Internet.

Finally, enjoy the rewards.
God has generously blessed me through the children who have sat with me on the steps of the altar. I marvel to see how young children can catch the meaning behind stories before I've even gotten to the explanations. I rejoice in the delightful insights of my young audiences. I suspect that, through the years, they have taught me far more than I have taught them.

May God bless you as you teach the children—and, in teaching them, welcome the Lord Jesus himself into your midst.

Making Room for Jesus

Preparation: Bring a doll's crib or a small manger filled with crumpled papers on which you've printed "worry and bad-attitude statements" ("Why can't I have that toy?" "What if she doesn't like me?" "I want my own way," "He makes me so mad," "I need to buy new clothes," "What if those kids pick on me?" etc.). Also bring a doll, representing the baby Jesus, wrapped in "swaddling cloths" and a blanket.

Today is the first Sunday in Advent. We can see one candle lit on the Advent wreath. It's also the first Sunday in the new church year. Even though most calendars start the new year on the first day of January, the church's new year starts on the first Sunday of Advent. Time is passing quickly; a new year has begun again.

Advent season is a time of waiting. We usually think of it as a time of waiting for Christmas—when Jesus came to the earth for the first time. The Bible verses that we read in church on the Sundays during Advent, however, remind us that it is also a time of waiting for Jesus to return once more to Earth.

In the reading from Luke, Jesus tells his friends to watch and be ready for him to return. Jesus says, "Watch out! Don't let me find you . . . filled with the worries of this life." During this season of Advent, Jesus says the same thing to us. "I'm coming back," he says. "Don't let me find you filled with the worries of this life."

I brought something very special with me this morning. *(Bring out or point to the manger filled with crumpled paper.)*

  *Scolding the Snakes*

This is a manger that I need to get ready for the baby Jesus. I can't very well use this the way it is, though. Why can't I put the baby Jesus in this crib? *(Let children respond.)* It's full of stuff, isn't it? What do we need to do to get the manger ready for Jesus? *(Let children respond.)* Yes! We need to clear out the manger to make room for the baby.

As we get ready for Advent, we want to make room in our hearts for Jesus. We need to clear out the things in our own lives that crowd out Jesus. Let's see what we have to take out of this manger to make room for Jesus. *(Read some words scribbled on the crumpled papers as you pitch them in a waste basket. Empty out manger.)*

Now that we've gotten rid of all that stuff, there's room in the manger for the baby Jesus. And when we get rid of all the worries and bad things in our hearts, we make room in our lives for Jesus. Now we can place the baby in our manger. *(Place doll in manger.)* This Advent, let's clean out all the bad and unkind and worried things in our lives to make room for Jesus.

We know you are with us, Lord Jesus; help us always to remember to keep our hearts clean and ready to be your home.

Notes

Dirt and Dross

Preparation: Cover a piece of smooth jewelry (a golden heart would be perfect) with mud or clay so that it is hidden inside the lump. Also bring a towel and bowl of water for cleaning the jewelry.

How many candles are lit on the Advent wreath now? *(Let kids count.)* Two candles! It's the second Sunday in Advent. This is a time of getting ready, isn't it? We remember that Jesus first came to Earth as a little baby born in Bethlehem about two thousand years ago. That was the first time Jesus came to Earth. Will Jesus come again? *(Children may respond.)* Yes, he will come again. We want to be ready for Christmas, but we also need to be ready for when Jesus returns.

At Christmastime we clean our homes and decorate them to get ready for guests or to have holiday parties. We also want to get our hearts and our lives ready to welcome Jesus. But if it were just up to us to make ourselves ready for Jesus, we could never do it, could we? We can't wash away our own sins. And we can't get rid of the bad thoughts in our heads. We can't do it by *ourselves*. We need to let Jesus wash away our sins and get rid of the bad things in our lives.

I have something with me that really needs some cleaning. *(Show your mud-caked treasure.)* I know that there is a beautiful treasure inside, but first I need to wash away all this dirt so that everyone can see it. We are like this lump of dirt with a treasure inside. God has created each one of us to be a special, talented person. But the bad things we do and the mean things we say sometimes cover up the beauty. We need to allow Jesus to wash us. If we ask Jesus to forgive us and to clean away all the sin from our lives, he will start working on us. *(Begin to clean your treasure in bowl.)*

The Old Testament book of Malachi says that Jesus' second coming will be like a refiner's fire. It says that Jesus will burn away all the dross, or sin and bad things, in our lives until the pure silver—the good part of us—shines through.

If you are a metalworker and you want to get a lump of pure silver, you need to get rid of everything in that chunk of metal that is not silver. A refiner's fire is very very hot, and it will remove everything that is not pure silver. Now Jesus doesn't *really* use fire to get rid of the bad things in our lives, but he does promise to help us change and become good followers—if we ask him to and then let him lead us. *(Show polished treasure to children.)*

Come, Lord Jesus. Wash away our sins and uncover your treasures. Help us get ready for you to come. Amen

Notes

Scolding the Snakes

Preparation: If possible, bring a rubber snake or a picture of a snake to illustrate the sermon.

Can you count the lighted candles on the Advent wreath? *(That's right: three. This is the third week of Advent.)* You remember that we said Advent is a time of getting ready. Who remembers what we are getting ready for? *(Let children answer.)* We want to be ready for Christmas, when Jesus was born, but we also need to be ready for when Jesus comes back.

Jesus was born long ago in Bethlehem, and when he was about thirty years old, Jesus was ready to begin telling people about God and about why he had come to live on Earth. But before Jesus began to teach and preach, God wanted to make sure the people were ready to listen. So God sent someone ahead of Jesus to get everyone ready. Do you know who that person was? *(Someone may answer.)*

A man named John the Baptist was sent to tell the people to get ready for Jesus. He was not a shy or quiet preacher. John the Baptist told people to get ready for Jesus by repenting. And he shouted it loud: "Repent!" To repent means to change your direction, to turn around. It means to stop doing the bad things that God doesn't like, and to start doing the things that God really wants you to do. What if we had the bad habit of hitting people every time we got angry? If we repent, then what happens? *(Let kids offer ideas.)* We stop hitting, don't we?

What if you told God that you were really sorry and promised to stop hitting other people, but in the back of your mind, you were thinking, "I'll stop hitting everyone except my sister. She makes me so mad." Does God know what you're thinking? Is that really repenting?

After hearing John the Baptist, lots of people said they would repent and change. Most of the people really did repent. But some people only wanted to *look* like they were following God. In their hearts, they didn't really want to change. John scolded those pretenders. Do you know what he called them? He called them poisonous snakes. *(Hold up rubber snake.)*

How do many people feel about snakes? *(Let children answer. Even though most snakes are harmless—even beneficial—some are poisonous and should not be approached or handled.)* Snakes are quiet and kind of sneaky. And some snakes—the bad ones—are filled with poison. John was angry with people who pretended to repent. They were like snakes: they were being sneaky with God; they were poisonous inside.

We all do things that are wrong sometimes, but once we know what needs to be changed, we must really want to change it. We don't want to be sneaky and false like snakes.

Forgive our sins, Lord Jesus, and change us to be more and more like you.

Notes

Leap for Joy

Today how many candles are lit on the Advent wreath? *(Children may respond.)* It's the fourth Sunday in Advent, isn't it? It's almost—*almost*—time for Christmas! We want to be ready for Christmas, and we want to be ready when Jesus comes to Earth again.

Is everyone ready? The Gospel lesson for today shows us two women who were ready for God's Son to come. Mary had just been told by the angel Gabriel that she was going to be the mother of Jesus, God's Son. The angel also told her that her cousin Elizabeth, who was very old and had never been able to have children, was pregnant. This was a lot of amazing news for Mary to take in, but Mary was ready. She believed what the angel said. She said she would be willing to be the mother of this special baby. Mary was ready for Christmas.

Mary's cousin Elizabeth was ready, too. Elizabeth was much older than most mothers, and she was having a baby for the first time. She knew something special was happening. God was at work. Elizabeth's son would be named John the Baptist, and he would help make the world ready for Jesus. Elizabeth was ready for Christmas.

Even the tiny baby inside Elizabeth—John the Baptist—was ready. Mary went to visit her cousin Elizabeth. And as soon as Mary stepped through the door and said, "Hello," the baby inside Elizabeth moved, and Elizabeth knew that Mary had a wonderful secret. God told her that Mary was going to be the mother of God's Son. Elizabeth told Mary, "The instant I heard your voice, my baby jumped for joy!

You are blessed because you believed the Lord's promise to you."

Mary was ready, Elizabeth was ready, even John the Baptist—who wasn't even born yet—was ready. The world was getting ready for Jesus, ready for the first Christmas. God was getting their hearts ready. All of these people were believing in God. Mary sang a song of joy, and the baby, John, leaped for joy. They were excited and happy.

We get excited before Christmas, don't we? As Christmas gets closer and closer, sometimes it's hard to hold all that excitement in. We just have to jump up and down or sing or yell. *(You may share a childhood memory of your own or an expression that shows your excitement.)* What do *you* do when you're really excited and happy? *(Let children share.)*

It's a good thing to be excited about Christmas! Jesus is coming! Let's all leap for joy! *(You may leap and yell, "Hooray!" with the children, or let the children leap for joy.)*

Jesus, we love you and can't wait to celebrate your birth once again. Thank you for coming to be born.

Notes

Light in the Dark

Preparation: Bring a strong flashlight and, if possible, arrange ahead of time to have an adult volunteer darken the church at one point during the sermon. (Agree on a signal to cue the volunteer.)

We have come to the end of Advent. The time of waiting is over. We stand at the beginning of Christmas. Tonight is a wonderful night: it is Christmas Eve. As the sun comes up tomorrow on Christmas morning, we will remember how our Savior Jesus was born as a tiny baby in our world.

Jesus is sometimes called the Light of the World. And at Christmas Jesus fills us all with light and joy. Jesus, the Light of the World, is with us now, but it still gets dark at nighttime. Jesus came to bring light to a different kind of darkness—the darkness that comes when we sin. When we sin and disobey God, it is as if we get lost and start stumbling around in the dark. We keep going the wrong way, keep hurting ourselves and others. And everything seems very, very dark. Then suddenly Jesus is here lighting our path. The light of Jesus pushes away the darkness of our sin and shows the way we should go.

Isaiah was a prophet who lived a long time ago, even long before Jesus was born. Isaiah knew that Jesus would come one day, and that Jesus would bring light to our world. Isaiah wrote, "The people who walk in darkness will see a great light—a light that will shine on all who live in the land where death casts its shadow" (Isa. 9:2 NLT).

What do you think it's like to walk in darkness? *(Kids can respond.)* I'd like one volunteer to go to the back of the church and stand in the aisle. *(Choose a child, then let him or her go to the back.)* Wave to us so we can see you. *(Wait for volunteer to get ready.)* Isaiah talked about people walking in the darkness, so that's what our volunteer in the back is going to try to do. We're going to turn off most of the lights, but before we do, let's hold hands. We don't want anyone to get lost or scared. *(Signal the adult to turn off as many lights as possible.)*

It's pretty dark now, isn't it? And if there were no light at all, it would be darker still. Would it be hard to walk very far in complete darkness? *(Let kids respond.)* I have something here that might help. *(Pull flashlight out of bag.)* What could we do to help the person at the back of the church walk through the darkness up to the front? *(Child that answers correctly may help shine light.)* This light makes a big difference! The light shows the way.

Jesus, thank you for being the light in our lives. You show us how to live and where to go. Thank you, God, for sending us the Light of the World at Christmas. Thank you for taking away the darkness of our sin. In Jesus' name. Amen

Notes

Jesus, the Word

Preparation: Bring an empty shoebox with a lid.

Christmas greetings! Today is a wonderful day, a day to celebrate! Today we remember how Jesus was born as a baby in a manger in Bethlehem. God sent his only Son down to Earth to live among us. If we could go back in time, we might be able to kneel at the manger and see the baby Jesus. We could see the beginning of God's amazing plan to save all of creation from sin.

If we could travel back even farther to the beginning of time, before the earth was created, what do you think we would see? *(Let kids offer ideas.)* We wouldn't see anything, would we? The universe was empty—no light, no stars, nothing. *(Bring out box with lid.)* This box has nothing inside. I'll open it and show you how empty it is. *(Open box and let kids look inside.)*

In the beginning, God spoke a word into the emptiness and created the world. Can I speak a word into this box and make something appear? *(Let children respond.)* Let's try it. I like butterflies, so I'll speak the word *butterflies* into this empty box and see if anything happens. *(Try it, then show empty box. Then let one or two children try with their own words.)* It isn't working, is it? We can't create something out of nothing.

If I were a magician, I might be able to make something appear in the box, and it might look like it appeared all by itself. But it would just be a trick. God's creation wasn't a trick, was it? The first chapter in the Gospel of John says, "In the beginning the Word . . . was with God, and he was God. He created everything there is. Nothing exists that he didn't make. . . . The Word became human and lived here on earth among us" (John 1:1-3, 14 NLT).

Can anyone tell me who "the Word" is? *(Someone may offer the answer.)* Jesus is "the Word." Jesus was there in the very beginning. He helped create everything. Then Jesus became one of us and walked on Earth with the things he helped create.

If one of you took this empty shoebox and made a picture or put some clay people inside, you would be a creator. You could look at your creation and enjoy what you had made. And if you made yourself really small, you could enter the scene you had made and be a part of it. That is just a little like what God did on the first Christmas. Our God, the creator of the universe, entered our world on Christmas as a little baby. The Word became human and came to live among us.

Lord, we thank and praise you for Christmas and for the best gift of all. Merry Christmas everyone!

Notes

Young Teacher

D o any of you have a favorite teacher, a teacher at school or Sunday school whom you really like a lot? *(If they wish, children can name some of their teachers.)* Teachers are wonderful, aren't they? They make learning fun and exciting. They make us happy to go to school. *(You may tell about one of your favorite teachers and what made that teacher special.)*

Jesus was a teacher. People often called him "Rabbi," which means "Teacher." Jesus was an excellent teacher. He used interesting stories to teach. He used examples from the world around him; he used things that people could see to teach about heaven and other things that people could not see. Jesus taught old people and young people. He taught people from many different countries and cultures. Most people know that Jesus was a great teacher.

But do you know how old Jesus was when he began to teach? *(Let children guess.)* Is anyone here twelve years old? *(Invite a twelve-year-old volunteer to stand up.)* This is how old Jesus was when he first began to teach at the temple in Jerusalem. He was only twelve years old, and already he was asking and answering difficult questions about God.

Are any of you teachers yet? *(Let kids respond.)* Well, you may not be teachers at a school, but children certainly are teachers at times.

Children teach grown-ups to stop and look closely at flowers and rocks. They teach bigger people to hunker down low so they can get a better view of a line of ants busily working. They teach us adults to stop and take time for really important things like snuggling and reading books.

There are so many things that kids like you can teach adults. From you we learn how to have fun and how to be surprised and curious and how to believe and trust.

Jesus is a great teacher, and we hope we'll always be willing to learn from him. But don't forget that you are teachers too! When you go back to your seats, you can ask your parents what you have taught them. Then talk about how you can learn together from Jesus.

Jesus, you are our very best teacher. Help us learn what you want us to be and do.

Notes

God's Word

Preparation: Bring along a large sheet of posterboard or a paper flipchart and a marking pen.

You can tell a lot about people from the words they speak. What do our words say about us? If we only speak loud, angry words or words that hurt others, we show everyone that we are angry inside. If we speak kind and gentle words or words that help others, we show everyone that we are full of kindness. The words that we speak show who we are and what we are like.

What about God's words? What kind of words does God say, and how do those words show us what God is like? I'd like to read to you some verses from the first chapter of John that talk about the Word of God. Listen carefully and try to tell me what the "Word" is.

"In the beginning was the Word, and the Word was with God, and the Word was God. He was in the beginning with God. All things came into being through him . . . *and the Word became a human being and came to live with us*, full of grace and truth" (John 1:1-3, 14, author's paraphrase).

Do you know who the Word is? *(Let children answer.)* It's Jesus! Jesus was there at the very beginning of the world. Everything was created through Jesus. Have you ever thought of Jesus as a word? Our words tell others what we are like. Jesus came here to Earth to show us what God is like, to teach us about God. What does God's "Word," Jesus, tell us about God? Can you think of some words to describe Jesus?

(Let kids come up with describing words such as loving, gentle, honest, or kind. *Write them down.)* Those are all words that describe God. Jesus, the Word of God, shows us what God is like.

What an amazing Word God sent to our world to teach us how much he loves us! He sent Jesus to us to save us from our sins. The Word of God is very important. God's Word, Jesus, tells us a lot about God.

The words we speak are important, too—the words we speak *about* God and *about* others, and the words we speak *to* others. Pay close attention to the words you speak today; they tell others a lot about you—and a lot about the God who loves us. Remember to choose your words carefully.

Guard our lips and our words, dear Lord, so that all we say gives honor and love to you.

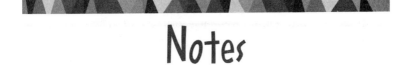

Notes

Burning the Chaff

Preparation: Bring a pan with clean popsicle sticks in the bottom covered by a fine layer of flour or other fine meal that can be blown away. You may print the following statements on the popsicle sticks: "Listen to God" and "Obey God."

Today is the first Sunday after the special day we call Epiphany. The season of Christmas has come to an end. On Epiphany we remember how the wise men followed a star to find the child Jesus.

Today we also remember the time when Jesus was baptized by his cousin John. Before Jesus came to him to be baptized, John had been baptizing people in the Jordan River. The people John baptized repented of their sins—that is, they said they were sorry and wanted to follow God.

Jesus didn't need to repent; his baptism was very special. But the other people who came to be baptized did need to repent. They knew they had not put God first in their lives, but they decided to change. Some might have decided to change after hearing what John said about the coming Messiah, Jesus. John said, "He will baptize you with the Holy Spirit and with fire. He is ready to separate the chaff from the grain with his winnowing fork. Then he will clean up the threshing area, storing the grain in his barn but burning the chaff with never-ending fire" (Luke 3:16-17 NLT).

Does it sound like it would be better to be the grain or the chaff? *(If necessary, read the second part of the above verse again. Discuss.)* The grain was stored in the barn. But what

　　　Scolding the Snakes

happened to the chaff? *(Children may answer.)* The chaff was the straw and tough husks that covered the grain. In order to separate chaff and grain, farmers used big forks to toss this mixture into the wind. The grain was heavier, so it fell down; but the wind blew away the lighter chaff, and it landed in a pile farther away. The pile of useless chaff was burned. The good grain was kept and made into bread and cakes.

The people who came to be baptized by John did not want to be like chaff. They wanted to be useful in God's kingdom. So they stopped doing things they knew they shouldn't and started to listen to God and to obey God.

I'd like to show you what the chaff was like. I have some messages written on sticks. But the sticks are covered up. I'll blow the "chaff" away and then show you the messages. *(Blow to remove flour; pass sticks around.)* When we disobey God, we are acting like chaff. We cannot be useful in God's kingdom if we don't obey him. But when we repent and start listening to God, we are like the precious grain.

Lord, help us to obey you, and forgive us when we fail.

Notes

Miracles vs. Magic

Preparation: Prepare a simple magic trick or use the trick described here. For this magic trick, you will need a small, clear glass jar containing 1 cup of water mixed with 1 teaspoon of ammonia; a paper bag; and a lid for the jar, in which you have placed a finely ground Ex-Lax tablet. Prior to the sermon, practice the trick several times so you can perform it smoothly.

Can anyone tell me the difference between a miracle and a magic trick? *(Let children try to respond.)* A miracle involves an amazing change—a real change—that happens by the power of God. A magic trick isn't real; it's done by a person to fool you into thinking something amazing happened. There is a big difference between magic and a real miracle.

Let me demonstrate a magic trick. *(Use your own simple magic trick or use my example.)* I have here a jar of clear water and a "magic" bag. You can see that there's nothing in my bag *(show the children)*, but when I place this jar of water in the magic bag and cover it, watch what happens. *(Grasp the top of the jar and place it in bag; then pick up lid and—out of view of children—quickly invert it so powder falls into the water. Screw the lid on firmly. The powdered tablet will turn the ammonia-water bright pink. Tip jar inside bag over and back to mix solution.)* Do you think my magic bag is working? Let's look inside and see. *(Pull jar out of bag to show that it has turned pink.)* Is this a miracle or a magic trick? *(Kids may respond, and you may explain how you did the trick.)* This was a fun trick, but it certainly wasn't a miracle.

Our Gospel lesson in John describes the very first miracle that Jesus did. He was with his mother at a wedding in a town called Cana. While they were celebrating, the host ran out of wine. There was nothing to give the guests to drink. The host was probably upset: weddings were very special occasions, and he wanted everything to be just right.

Then Jesus did something amazing. He told the servants to fill six large stone jars with fresh water. They did exactly as he told them, and then they dipped a cup out of one of the jars and took it to the host so that he could taste it. The water had been changed into wine; and not only that, it was very good wine. The host was amazed and very happy.

Now, do you think that was a magic trick or did something really change by the power of God? *(Discuss.)* This was truly a miracle. The water actually turned into wine. This was a sign to the people that Jesus was special, that he really was God's promised Savior. God does not work magic, God performs real miracles.

Jesus, we know that you are truly God's Son. By your power, you have forgiven our sins and changed us into good people, people who love and serve you. Thank you.

Notes

The Body of Christ

What do you think is the most important part of your body? *(Let children share ideas; challenge their choices.)* If you had strong muscles but no nerves to send signals to your brain, would you be able to do anything with those muscles? No! If you had good eyes and could see the tiniest thing from far away, but your eyelids wouldn't stay open, would you be able to see anything? No! If you had a good brain, but your hands or eyes didn't do what the brain told them to do, would your brain do you any good? No! Every part of the body is important. And it is important for all the parts of the body to work together in order to do the things you need to do.

The people in this church are the body of Christ. *(Point around—at children, at adults: "She is part of Christ's body; you are part of Christ's body; they are part of Christ's body.")* All of us do the work of Jesus here on Earth. And just as the human body has many important parts that need to work together, the church has many members who are good at doing different things. Would it make sense if all of us were Sunday school teachers? Who would go to class and learn? What if all of us were ushers? We'd all be in the aisles and no one would be sitting in the seats.

Do you think the children in this congregation are a very important part of the body of Christ? *(Discuss.)* You are very important. We need you in our church. Your part in the body of Christ is very important. What are some important things you do for Jesus? *(Let children discuss. If necessary, supply examples: show kindness, smile, and help one another, tell others about Jesus, sing hymns, obey parents and teachers, etc.)*

Sometimes we might be tempted to think that some people or some jobs in the church are more important than others. But this is not at all what the Bible teaches! First Corinthians 12 talks about how all the members in Christ's body are important. It says, "In fact, some of the parts that seem weakest and least important are really the most necessary" (v. 22).

The way that one person feels can affect the whole body of Christ. If you break your pinky toe, you may not be able to walk at all for awhile. A toe is such a small thing, but if it is hurt, it affects your whole body. If one of the members of our church is sad or hurting, it matters to all of us. That's why we pray for one another and meet together and encourage one another. That's why we say good things to one another and tell others how helpful they are, how much they mean to us. Before you go home today, make sure that you talk to another part of this body of Christ and see how he or she is feeling.

We are all your children, Jesus—and each of us has important work to do for you. Help us remember that and help us love one other and work with one another. Amen

Notes

A Love Story

Preparation (Optional): Bring a stuffed dog and cat or a picture to illustrate the story.

Would you like to hear a love story? Don't worry; there's no kissing in this one. This is a story about an old dog and a little kitten. (*If you brought the stuffed animals, use them to help you tell the story.*)

Once upon a time, there was an old dog who really knew what it was to love. He was patient and kind and very happy when something good happened to someone else, even if it didn't happen to him. The dog was never rude and didn't brag when he had done something good. He was a very loving dog.

One day, a kitten wandered into the life of this dog. He found her cowering behind a garbage can. She was all dirty and half-starved. The kitten, though she needed help, was frightened of the dog. And she hissed and spat when the dog came near. The dog was very patient, though, and even though the kitten scratched his nose and bit his ears, he gently carried it over to his own bowl of food and let it eat every last crumb. The kitten had a full tummy now and was stronger; and when the dog tried to wash its matted fur by licking the kitten, it snapped at the dog and scratched him even harder. But the old dog's love was patient and kind. It was not irritable. The old dog's love did not insist on its own way. So the dog kept caring for the kitten.

Other dogs came around and looked at the raggedy kitten scratching the old dog every time he tried to help, and

they told him, "Why do you bother with that dirty little kitten? Look at all the scratches it has given you! You should give up on it." But the old dog's love never gave up, never lost faith, and it lasted through every difficulty. So the dog kept caring for the kitten.

By the end of a week, the dog had a very sore nose and chewed-up ears, but the kitten looked much better. Its fur was clean and groomed and soft. Its little belly was plump. Its whiskers were straight, and its eyes were bright.

And the next time the other dogs came around, there sat the loving old dog: his scratches were healed, and he was happily curled around a little purring ball of a kitten. The old dog had not only saved the kitten's life, he had also taught it how to love.

What do you think made that kitten change? How did the old dog teach the kitten about love? (*Let children answer.*) When you get home today, have your parents read 1 Corinthians 13 to you. It will teach you about love.

Lord, teach us to love you more and more, and help us love one another just as you love us.

Notes

Fishers of People

Preparation: Bring a fishing net or large basket.

When Jesus began preaching and teaching people about God, he also asked special followers (we call them his disciples) to help him spread the good news about God's love. One of the first disciples to follow Jesus was a man named Simon Peter. Do you know what Simon Peter did for a living? *(Let children respond.)* He was a fisherman, wasn't he? He took a fishing boat out onto the Sea of Galilee with some other fishermen, and they would throw their big nets into the water. *(You may demonstrate with the net or basket.)* Fish would swim into the nets, and then the fishermen would pull in the nets. If the fishermen were lucky, they had quite a few fish in their nets. Sometimes, though, they only caught a few little fish or none at all.

One day, Jesus got into Simon Peter's boat and asked Simon to row out a little way from the shore. Then Jesus stood up in the boat and talked to the huge crowd of people on the beach. Just to be sure they could all hear him well, Jesus stood in the boat and preached from the lake.

When Jesus had finished teaching, he told Simon to go out into the deep water and let the fishing nets down. Even though the fishermen had not caught a single fish all night and all morning, Simon and his friends did what Jesus told them. And, as soon as they let down their nets, they found that the nets were so full of fish they could hardly pull them in. They had to get another boat to help them!

Simon Peter was so surprised! Jesus had done a wonderful miracle. Suddenly Peter realized that Jesus was truly the Son of God, and he fell to his knees right there in the boat. Jesus told Simon, "Don't be afraid. From now on, you'll be fishing for people!" (Luke 5:10 NLT). Jesus didn't mean that Simon Peter would be catching people with his fishing net; he meant that he would be bringing people into God's kingdom by telling everyone about Jesus.

When you invite someone to church or tell them about Jesus, it's sort of like casting a net to catch fish. You're trying to pull them toward God. But if you try to do it all alone, you're a bit like Simon when he fished all night and caught nothing. When Jesus helped the fishermen, their nets were full of fish. Those fish didn't just happen to be waiting there all packed together. Jesus called them to the nets.

And Jesus promises to help us, too, when we "fish for people." If we do our part, telling people about God's love and inviting them to church, God will do his part and help our words and help those people to believe in him. Good fishing to all of you!

Dear God, help us to catch people for you and your kingdom!

Notes

Blessed Are the Poor

Preparation (Optional): Bring a large flipchart of paper and a marker to write with.

This morning I'd like you to help me think of reasons why it might be a good thing to be poor. We'll write them down. *(Let children offer ideas. They may have trouble, so you can help by asking leading questions. Make notes on chart.)* If you didn't have many toys, would you have to clean your room as often? If you only had one set of clothes, would it be easy to decide what to wear? And, if you didn't have much food, you would really be thankful for the food you had, wouldn't you?

Do you know what Jesus said about being poor? Jesus said, "God blesses you who are poor, for the kingdom of God is given to you" (Luke 6:20 NLT). Many people think it's a great thing to be rich, to be able to buy anything they want. Lots of times we think this way, too, don't we?

Maybe Jesus knows something that we don't. If you don't have a lot of stylish clothes or toys filling up your life, maybe it's easier for God to get your attention. If you don't give the love in your heart to a fancy house or giant Lego set *(or substitute current popular toys and games)*, maybe it's easier to give God the love in your heart. And maybe it's easier for us to understand other people who don't have very much.

Now, can you tell me why it might be a bad thing to be rich? *(Open a clean sheet of paper on flipchart. Again, help children with leading questions.)* If you're rich, you have to pay lots of taxes. If you're rich, would you have to protect your things from being stolen? *And,* you might even start loving all those nice things more than you love God or more than you love other people.

Do you know what Jesus said about the rich? He said, "What sorrows await you who are rich, for you have your only happiness now" (Luke 6:24 NLT). So the rich may be happy in this world now, but does our life end here on this earth? Those who believe in Jesus are promised a home in heaven, a place better than anything riches could buy here on Earth. Of course, there are lots of rich people who love God with all their heart. And there are poor people who do not love God. But it's when we think riches are so very important—when we think we could be happy if only we were rich—that we might forget about God and others. That is what Jesus was warning us against.

So the next time you're tempted to think money and riches are the most important things in the world, remember the words of Jesus: "God blesses you who are poor, for the kingdom of God is given to you."

Help us to remember that you are the most important thing in the world, dear Jesus.

Notes

Giving God's Way

Preparation: Bring two bowls, both half full of a pourable grain such as rice, measuring cups, and a funnel.

This morning let's talk about giving and receiving. How many of you have ever given away things of your own to make others happy? If you give things to others, do you think others ought to give something back to you, too? (*Let kids talk about this.*) Do you think that giving and receiving should be even—that the amount that we give should be given back to us in the same measure? Many people feel that this is only fair.

Let's show how a fair exchange should work. (*Scoop up one cup of rice.*) If Bowl A gives one cup of rice to Bowl B, then sometime Bowl B should give one cup of rice back to Bowl A. (*Demonstrate this with your cups of rice.*) Both of the bowls think this is fair. You should get back what you give. The bowls should end up staying pretty even. This is how the world figures things should work out. This seems fair.

But God has a different way of looking at giving and receiving. God tells us to give *without expecting anything in return*. We are to love others without thinking of ourselves. Do you think that if we really do this, if we give and give and give, we might end up without anything—with an empty bowl? (*Let kids respond.*) God's ways are not our ways, and with God some very surprising things happen.

I'm going to take a cup of something that I can give to others. (*Scoop up a cup of rice.*) This cup represents the time that I

give to my church and neighborhood doing God's work. Let's say I give one cup of my time and talent to the Lord. I'll pour it into the Lord's bowl here. And I'm not worried about running out, nor am I expecting that I'll get anything back. *(Pour your cup of rice into the other bowl.)*

Now what do you suppose happens? *(Children may answer.)* The Lord will always outgive us. *(Put your empty cup back into your bowl and start to pour the rice from the other bowl into your cup so that it fills the cup and then overflows into your bowl.)* Every time we give of our lives to God—without expecting anything back—God will give us so much goodness and joy that our lives overflow with God's love.

In Luke, chapter 6, Jesus says, "If you forgive others, you will be forgiven. If you give, you will receive. Your gift will return to you in full measure, pressed down, shaken together to make room for more, and running over" (vv. 37-38 NLT). When we give to God—to others for God's sake—God does not give back to us the same amount. He gives back so much that our blessings overflow, and we can't help but bless others with the extra.

We praise you, God, because all blessings come from you—and you give us more than we need.

Notes

Follow the Leader

Preparation: Bring a blindfold that will fit over a child's eyes.

Have any of you ever played "follow the leader"? How do you play? (*Let kids explain; you may summarize.*) One person is the leader, and everyone else lines up behind that person and does exactly as the leader does, right? Let's try a quick game. I'll be the leader. (*Quickly lead the group in a brief walk of silly steps and hand motions.*)

That was fun, wasn't it? Do you think you would be able to play "follow the leader" if everyone was blindfolded? What might happen? (*Children may share. Try blindfolding a person and asking her to lead. But be sure to stop the game quickly so nobody stumbles or gets hurt. Then discuss this blind leading.*) If we can't see, how do we know how to follow, what to do? And if the leader can't see, how can she know where to go or what to do? If nobody can see, someone might get hurt. You wouldn't be safe even if you were holding hands. The leader might not see a deep ditch or a cliff in front of her, and then when she fell over the edge, everyone would fall over with her. You especially would not want your leader to be blindfolded. The leader has to be able to see where she is going.

In Luke, chapter 6, Jesus said, "What good is it for one blind person to lead another? The first one will fall into a ditch and pull the other down also. A student is not greater than the teacher. But the student who works hard will become like the teacher" (vv. 39-40 NLT). Jesus is trying to tell us that we have to be careful who we follow in life. If we are following the advice of one of our friends who has bad ideas—like wanting to steal things or say bad words or hurt other people—it's like following a blindfolded leader. That person will pull you down and get you into trouble.

Jesus wants us to follow good examples and good teachers. Our parents can teach us the right way to go. Our pastors and Sunday school teachers can be good leaders. And the best teacher of all is Jesus. If we listen to what Jesus says and try to follow where he leads us as we grow up, we will become more and more like him. Then when we have learned a lot from Jesus, we can be good leaders, too.

When we play "follow the leader" with our friends, it can be just a fun game. But when you choose the leader who will direct your whole life, I pray that you will choose Jesus. He will always lead you the right way.

Jesus, you are our leader. Help us to follow where you lead.

Notes

A Glimpse of Glory

Today is Transfiguration Sunday. *Transfiguration* means to change the way something or someone looks. On this day, we remember how Jesus went up on a mountaintop with his disciples and showed them just how special he was.

Jesus had told his disciples, his close friends, that he would be killed and later rise from the dead. How do you think the disciples looked when Jesus told them that bad things were going to happen to him? Show me how the faces of the disciples must have looked. *(Let the kids act out the sad emotions.)* They must have been very, very sad.

Eight days after he had told them this, he chose three of his disciples, Peter, James, and John to climb up a mountain with him. Let's all pretend we're climbing together. *(Pantomime climbing motions.)* Whew! Let's sit down and rest like the disciples did when they got to the top. *(Sit down together on steps or floor.)* Jesus took the disciples with him up that mountain to pray, but the disciples were very tired. The disciples prayed with him for awhile. Let's all pray like the disciples. *(Fold your hands with children.)* But pretty soon those tired disciples fell asleep. Show me how you can fall asleep on the ground. *(Let kids act out sleeping.)*

While Jesus was praying, his face and clothing began to glow like a light was shining inside him. His clothing turned white and glowed brightly. Two famous prophets, Moses and Elijah—men who had lived many, many years earlier—suddenly were right there talking to Jesus. The disciples woke up and saw the brightness and glory of Jesus, and they saw the two prophets talking with him. They were so surprised, they couldn't speak.

What do you think the disciples looked like when they saw Jesus glowing and those old prophets standing in front of them? Show me what they might have looked like. *(Make a look of amazement on your face and invite kids to do the same.)* I'm sure that this was a day that those disciples remembered for the rest of their lives.

Jesus was showing his disciples that he was truly special, that he was the Son of God. How do you think that made them feel about him? *(Let children answer.)* Jesus wanted to remind them that no matter what might happen, and no matter how sad they might feel or how bad things might seem, Jesus was very, very special. He was God's Son. He would always be there to help them. This is what we remember and celebrate on Transfiguration Sunday.

Jesus, thank you for always being nearby to love and help us. Remind us over and over again how very special you are and how very lucky we are.

Notes

Saved by Believing

A t most beaches and pools there is a person who sits in a tall chair and watches swimmers in the water. If someone in the water calls for help, this person jumps in the water and saves the person in danger. Can you tell me what this person is called? *(Children may answer.)* He or she is the lifeguard. The lifeguard's job is to make sure swimmers are safe.

Imagine that you're at the beach. Big waves are rolling in and crashing against some large boulders. It's a wonderful place to explore, and you're climbing this way and that, investigating the tide pools and looking at starfish and little crabs. A lifeguard is sitting in a tall chair watching over all the people. The lifeguard tells everyone, "If you're ever in trouble and want me to come and save you, all you have to do is yell, 'Help!' and I'll come right away."

So you know what to do if you have any trouble at the beach. But what if there is one girl at that same beach who thinks she can handle anything—that she can always take care of herself. This girl figures that she won't ever need help from anyone. So she wades through the water, tries to squeeze between two rocks, and gets stuck! She's not big enough to move one of the rocks and free herself; she needs somebody to help. The lifeguard can't see the girl because she's behind the big boulder. The tide is coming in and the water is getting deeper and deeper. What should the girl do? *(Let kids offer suggestions.)*

If she calls for help, the lifeguard will come right away and save her. What if this girl isn't the lifeguard's sister—what if she isn't related to the lifeguard at all—will the lifeguard still save her? *(Kids may help in answering.)* Yes, of course. What if she isn't a friend of the lifeguard? Will the lifeguard still save her? What if the girl in trouble is from a different country? Will the lifeguard still save her? Anyone who calls out for help will be saved by the lifeguard. But what if the girl doesn't call out for help? What if she were too stubborn to ask for help? Can the lifeguard save her? Probably not.

When we sin and do bad things, it's kind of like we're drowning. We feel worse and worse, but it's like we just can't stop ourselves. We're like the girl caught in the rocks: we need a lifeguard to help save us. The Bible tells us how to be saved from our sins. In Romans, chapter 10, the Bible says, "Everyone who calls on the name of the Lord will be saved" (v. 13 NIV).

It's that simple. Ask God to forgive you and help you, and God will. God will save you from your sins. It doesn't matter who you are; you just have to ask.

Lord Jesus, you are our lifeguard. You have promised to forgive us whenever we ask. Help us to ask.

Notes

The Fox and the Hen

Preparation: Bring pictures of a fox and/or a hen and baby chicks to illustrate talk.

In today's Gospel lesson from Luke, we are told that some leaders of the Jewish people (called Pharisees) came to Jesus after he had finished preaching to a crowd of people. They told him, "You'd better get out of here if you want to live, because Herod Antipas wants to kill you." Herod was the ruler of the land, and he was powerful. But Jesus answered, "Go tell that fox that I will keep on casting out demons and doing miracles of healing . . ." (Luke 13:32 NLT).

Jesus called Herod a fox. Why do you suppose he would call someone a fox? What do you think Herod was like? *(Kids can give their ideas.)* Foxes are hunters. They kill other animals for their food. Foxes also can be very sneaky. Many farmers don't like foxes, because foxes love to kill chickens. And foxes don't just kill for food; often times they will get into a chicken house and kill chickens just for the fun of it. Jesus called Herod a fox, so Herod probably wasn't a very nice person.

If a fox sneaked into a chicken house and met a mother hen in there with her little chicks, what do you suppose would happen? Would the hen run away or fly away from the fox to save her life? *(Let children respond.)* No, even if the hen were very frightened, she would stay to protect her chicks. If the fox attacked, the hen would spread out her wings, and all the chicks would run to her and hide under her wings. Then the hen would peck at the fox, trying to drive it off with her sharp beak. The mother hen never leaves her chicks, even if it means that she might be killed.

After Jesus called Herod a fox, he looked out over the city of Jerusalem and said, "O Jerusalem, Jerusalem, the city that kills the prophets and stones God's messengers! How often I have wanted to gather your children together as a hen protects her chicks beneath her wings, but you wouldn't let me" (Luke 13:34 NLT).

Jesus says that he is like a mother hen. What do you think he means? How is Jesus like a mother hen? (*Let children respond.*) How can Jesus protect us from danger? (*Kids may respond.*)

Jesus was willing to lay down his life for us—to die to save us from sin and death. When Jesus died on the cross, he died for the wrong things that *we* do, so that we don't have to. Jesus covers us and protects us like a mother hen protects her chicks. All we have to do is go to him and let him save us and forgive us for our sins.

Lord, always keep us safe beside you. Help us never to wander away from your protecting wings.

Notes

Food for the Soul

Preparation: Bring brief, favorite Bible verses printed on cards or bookmarks—enough to give one to each child. If possible, also bring a flipchart and marker to jot down kids' responses.

What do all people and animals need to survive? *(Let children share thoughts. If you have a marker and chart, note their answers.)* We need food and water. We also need to stay warm. Animals have fur and feathers to keep them warm. How do people stay warm? Clothes and homes help keep people warm. So, we need food and clothing and homes. Do we need anything else to live?

Can baby animals that come from eggs survive all by themselves? *(Let children speculate.)* Some baby animals manage pretty well by themselves soon after they are hatched. Tiny turtles race for the ocean after they hatch from eggs; little alligators don't need much help; even some birds can start taking care of themselves soon after leaving their eggs.

But we don't hatch from eggs, do we? Just like monkeys and cats and dogs, we're born from our mommies. And babies like us need help to survive. We need to drink milk, and we need to be protected. Our parents find food for us. Humans take a long time to grow up. People are often about eighteen years old before they can survive on their own.

But you know, it's not just food and water and shelter that people and animals need to survive. If a baby doesn't get love and hugs, he or she may not survive. If a baby mammal in a zoo loses its mother, the zookeepers feed it, and they

  Scolding the Snakes

also snuggle and hold the little baby animal to make sure it stays healthy. People need lots of love to stay healthy, too. Where do we get love and hugs and snuggles? (*Let children answer.*)

People also need a special kind of food to stay healthy and happy on the inside. In the Old Testament book of Isaiah, we hear God's voice calling to us to come and eat and drink. "Is anyone thirsty? Come and drink—even if you have no money! . . . It's all free! . . . Listen, and I will tell you where to get food that is good for the soul!" (55:1-2 NLT).

Jesus is sometimes called the Bread of Life: the love he gives us and the things he teaches us help us to grow into strong, happy people. And Jesus is free for the asking. We need God's love for our souls to survive; and we need the Word of God, the Bible, to feed our lives—way past the age of eighteen. (*Hand out the bookmarks/Bible verses.*) Here is some food for your souls. Take these home and then snuggle up to your parents as you read the message together.

Thank you for giving us all we need to grow healthy and strong, Lord. Help us learn more and more about you by reading your words in the Bible.

Notes

Lost Dog

Preparation: Bring a poster or flyer with a picture and notice about a lost dog. Or make up your own poster for class.

H ave any of you ever seen a paper like this posted in your neighborhood? *(Hold up lost-dog poster for all children to see.)* Can you see what it is? Why do people put these notices up? *(Let children discuss the poster.)*

When someone loses a pet they really love, it is almost like losing a member of the family. The pet's owners will search for that lost pet day after day until they find their pet again. Sometimes they even offer a reward.

(You may share your own lost-pet story or use the following paragraph.) I feel sorry for any family that has lost a pet. If I see a sign like this, I keep my eyes open for a pet that looks like that. It would feel wonderful to be able to bring a lost pet back to its family again, wouldn't it?

The story in the Gospel today tells about a son who had left home and was living a miserable life. He had spent all his money. He had done some very bad and very foolish things. He didn't have a proper home, and he didn't have enough food to eat. He was so unhappy. In a way, he was lost.

The young man's father was very worried about him. This was the child he had kissed and fed and hugged and loved since the young man was a baby. A lost child is an awfully sad thing. But this story has a happy ending. The lost son finally decided to return home. When he came back to his father, he looked terrible, ragged, dirty, and hungry. He

       Scolding the Snakes

was afraid he wouldn't be welcomed home. But as soon as his father saw his son coming, he ran to him, hugged him, and threw a big party to celebrate his return. How do you think that lost son felt when he got back home? (*Let children describe.*)

Sometimes it seems like people feel sorrier for lost dogs than they do for lost people. It may be easier for us to care about a poor, ragged dog than to care about a poor, ragged human. Lost people take a lot more work. They may not look as cute as lost dogs, they may not ask for our help, they even may say mean things to us. But anytime people are unhappy or lonely or sinful—anytime they feel far away from God—they are lost children of the Lord. And they need our help to come home to God.

Jesus used to hang around with lost people when he lived on Earth. This was why Jesus came—to guide the lost children back to the heavenly Father. And our job as Christians is to tell people about God, to help bring them back to God. You are God's search and rescue team.

Jesus, make us your search and rescue team; help us bring lost people home to you. Amen

Notes

Giving Our Best

Preparation: Bring a reproduction of a religious work of art (from a poster, book, or magazine). It would be nice if this were a biblical scene the students might recognize.

'd like each of you to imagine that you are a famous artist. You've been practicing your drawing and painting for a long, long time. Now you can draw whatever you can picture in your mind. If you want to draw a galloping horse, you can do it so well that it almost looks as if the horse is moving on the paper. If you want to paint a picture of a flower in the morning sunshine, you can paint it so well that anyone could almost smell the flower's fragrance.

Now, imagine that Jesus himself asked you to paint a picture that he could hang up in heaven. What would you paint for Jesus? *(Let children offer ideas.)* You would want to paint a beautiful picture, wouldn't you? How long do you think it would take to finish your painting? *(Let children respond.)* You would want this painting to be the best you had ever done, wouldn't you? Here is a painting that one artist made to honor Jesus. He worked hard on it, and it is beautiful. *(Show painting and let children tell what it shows, how it makes them feel.)*

The Gospel lesson for today is from the book of John. It tells us about a woman who gave the very best that she had for Jesus. Jesus was eating dinner in the home of his friends Mary and Martha. Both these women loved Jesus very much. To show how much she loved him, Mary took a jar of very expensive perfume and poured it on Jesus' feet and then wiped his feet with her hair. One of the other guests said Mary was wrong to do this. He said she was wasteful, that she should have sold the perfume and given the money to the poor.

But Jesus stuck up for Mary. It was good that she wanted to show Jesus how much she loved him. Jesus knew that he would soon die on the cross, and he said to the man who criticized Mary: "Leave her alone. . . . You will always have the poor among you, but I will not be with you much longer" (John 12:7-8 NLT).

Mary was giving her very best for Jesus. It would be like us painting the very best picture we possibly could to give to Jesus. But you don't have to be an artist to give Jesus your best. What are some of the best things *you* can give Jesus? (*Let kids name talents or acts of kindness or service they can offer. If necessary, start them off: "Timmy, you can read really well; maybe you could read a story about Jesus to your little sister," or "Jenny, what could you do to honor Jesus by helping out at home?" etc.*)

All of us honor Jesus by living our lives to his glory by saying and doing things that show how much we love Jesus.

Jesus, help us to give you our very, very best in the way we live and in the way we act toward one another.

Notes

Shouting Stones

Preparation: Bring in palm branches and several large, smooth rocks to pass around or enough small stones to distribute to all the children.

Who can tell me what these are? *(Hold up rocks and let children answer.)* I'm going to pass around these rocks. As soon as you get one, I want you to hold it up to your ear and listen carefully. Tell me if you hear anything. When you're finished passing around the rocks, I want to talk to you about some special rocks. *(Allow time for rocks to go around and then collect them again. Let children report what they heard.)*

Today is Palm Sunday, when we remember how Jesus rode into the city of Jerusalem on a donkey. The crowds saw Jesus coming and spread their coats and blankets on the road to make a soft and colorful path. They also cut palm branches and waved them and shouted as Jesus approached. "Blessed is the king who comes in the name of the Lord! Peace in heaven, and glory in the highest heaven!" (Luke 19:38 NRSV).

Now, there were some Pharisees in the crowd—very proper people who were quite proud of themselves. And these Pharisees said to Jesus, "You should control your followers! Tell them to stop shouting and cheering for you like that" (Luke 19:39, author's paraphrase).

Do you know what Jesus said to them? He said, "If [the people] kept quiet, the very stones along the road would burst into cheers!" (Luke 19:40 NLT)

Wouldn't that be something? Can you imagine one of those rocks suddenly shouting, "Hurrah for Jesus!"? Did any of you hear the rocks yelling this morning? *(Let kids answer.)* The rocks were very quiet, weren't they? Now remember that Jesus said *if the people kept quiet and didn't praise the Lord,* the stones would cheer. But the people didn't keep quiet, did they? What did they say and do? *(Let children answer: they waved branches and cloaks and shouted praises.)*

And even today, people aren't keeping quiet about Jesus. We praise him every Sunday in church; we tell our friends about him; we sing songs about Jesus. All over the world, people are praising Jesus. So the stones don't have to burst into cheers.

Just to make sure these rocks don't have to start cheering, let's try a few "Hosannas" ourselves. *(Hand out palm leaves and lead children in waving palms and shouting, "Hosanna!")*

Optional: Give every child a stone to take with him or her. When they get home, they can paint a shouting face on it to remind them of Palm Sunday.

We praise and thank and worship you, Lord Jesus. You are our King, and we love you a lot!

Notes

The Last Enemy

Preparation: Bring a bouquet of colorful spring flowers and a vase in which to place them on the altar or at the foot of the cross.

Happy Easter everyone! Do you know the words to the Easter greeting that has been used in the Christian church for almost two thousand years? When I say to you, "The Lord is risen!" you answer back, "He is risen indeed! Hallelujah!"

You have to sound really loud and happy when you answer, because it is such good news. Let's try it. "The Lord is risen!" *(Children answer, "He is risen indeed! Hallelujah!" Try this several times so that children get the chance to sound really happy.)*

(Hold up the flowers you brought in.) I brought a bouquet of flowers because it's such a special day. When people have won a victory or done something great, they are often given flowers. It's a way to congratulate them, to say, "Way to go!"

Jesus did something really great, didn't he? What do we celebrate on Easter? *(A child may answer.)* Jesus died on the cross to take away our sins, and three days later, on Sunday, Jesus came back to life—he rose from the dead. Jesus beat death; it was a great victory! That's why we celebrate Easter.

God's people, the Israelites, had many enemies through-out their history. For a time, the Egyptians were enemies, but God helped the Israelites escape slavery in Egypt. God's people had another victory when the walls of an enemy city called Jericho came tumbling down. The Philistines were enemies, too, but when young David killed the Philistine giant Goliath, the Israelites had another victory. With God's help, the Israelites were able to defeat many enemies, but there was one enemy they could not defeat.

Ever since the beginning, when Adam sinned, the enemy that could not be beaten was death. The winners of every battle and every war finally grew old and died. Death always came in the end. But Jesus changed all that. Jesus took on the final enemy of God's people, and he won! We no longer have to be afraid of death. Our bodies still will get old and die, but we will come alive again—to live forever with God. And one day we will all be together living happily in heaven with God. Death has no power over us. Jesus won the battle.

Could I have a volunteer to help place these victory flowers on the altar? *(Choose one or two helpers to place flowers on altar or at foot of empty cross.)* Thank you. Happy Easter. Let's say the Easter greeting just one more time. And this time, let's invite everybody in church to join in the answer: "The Lord is risen!" *(Have congregation join in the response: "He is risen indeed! Hallelujah!")*

Thank you, Jesus, for giving us life with you that never ends.

Notes

Not Seeing but Believing

Preparation: Bring a paper fan (one you've purchased or made yourself) and a small whistle.

How many of you have heard the expression, "I'd have to see it to believe it"? Maybe some of you have used that expression yourselves. Let's say your brother is learning how to skateboard, and one day he comes running in to tell you that he can do an amazing trick on the skateboard. You might say, "I'd have to see that to believe it!" And until you actually see him perform the trick on the skateboard, you won't believe he can actually do it.

Do we always have to be able to see things in order to believe they exist? What are some things that we can't see but still know are there? *(Let kids share their thoughts.)* We can't see the air all around us, but when the wind is blowing, we can feel the air, or we can see the things it moves. *(Use fan to illustrate air movement—maybe letting it move a scrap of paper.)* We can't see sound waves, but when we hear a loud noise *(use whistle to illustrate sound)*, we know that sound is real. We can't see the love that our parents and friends have for us, but we feel their hugs and hear their loving words, and we know that their love is real.

Can we see Jesus—the *real* Jesus, not just pictures of him? *(Let kids respond.)* How do we know he's real? *(Children may share their thoughts.)* We believe what the Bible says. We feel Jesus' love in our hearts. And we can see the way people change—the way they become kinder and happier—when they believe in Jesus and let him into their lives. We can't say that we have seen Jesus with our own eyes. Still, we believe in him.

Today's Gospel lesson from the book of John tells the story of a disciple named Thomas, who did not believe Jesus came back to life. Jesus rose from the dead and appeared to his other disciples, but Thomas wasn't with them; he didn't see Jesus. Thomas would not believe that Jesus was alive unless he could see Jesus and touch him.

Then, some days after Jesus rose from the dead, the disciples were together again—and this time Thomas was with them. Suddenly Jesus appeared, and he told Thomas to touch the nail wounds in his hands and feel the spear wound in his side. Jesus wanted Thomas to stop doubting. Finally Thomas believed. Jesus said, "You believe because you have seen me. Blessed are those who haven't seen me and believe anyway" (John 20:29 NLT).

You are blessed. All of us are blessed. We have not seen or touched Jesus, but still we believe that Jesus is alive.

Jesus, thank you for being alive and for being here with us. And thank you for helping us to believe that you will always be with us. Amen

Notes

Feed My Lambs

Preparation: Bring a plastic bottle filled with water, and set it in plain view a short distance, but out of reach, from where you will sit with the children.

C an one of you tell me the name of someone you love? *(Call on several volunteers.)* What sorts of things do you do to show these people that you really love them? *(Let volunteers share.)* There are lots of things we can do to show people we love them. Your parents love you very much. What kinds of things do they do for you that show their love? *(Let children describe.)* When we care about someone, we can't help but do nice things for them. When we love people, we help them, don't we? And that's especially important when our loved ones can't do something by themselves and need our help.

Let's pretend right now, that my legs don't work and I am really thirsty. I can't get up and get my water bottle over there. *(Indicate water bottle.)* How do you suppose I could get that water? *(Let children offer suggestions until one gets the hint and goes to get the water for you.)* I can't reach the water, though some of you can. And now someone has gone to get the water for me. Thank you. *(Take a drink of water and then continue.)*

We could have talked for a long time about how you all would be able to help me, but if nobody had gotten up to get the water, I'd still be thirsty, right? After Jesus had risen from the dead, he appeared to his disciples several times.

One of the last times he was with them, he asked Simon Peter a question. "Simon, son of John," Jesus said, "do you love me?" "Yes, Lord," Peter replied, "you know I love you." "Then feed my lambs," Jesus told him. Jesus repeated his question three times, so it must have been very important. (John 21:15-17 NLT).

Do you know what Jesus was really telling Peter? Peter knew. Jesus was really talking about people. "Feed my lambs" means "help my people." The world is full of people who are hungry to hear the good news that Jesus came to save them from the bad things in their hearts. But if people who *know* about Jesus—people like Peter and like us—never share that good news, it is like a water bottle that is out of reach. The news won't do them any good. Somebody has to be willing to talk about Jesus to these hungry people. We feed Jesus' lambs when we tell people about God.

Lord Jesus, help us to feed your lambs. Help us to tell people about your love. In your name we pray. Amen

Notes

The Shepherd's Voice

How many of you answer the telephone in your home? *(Let kids raise their hands.)* Now, tell me this: how many of you have answered the phone and guessed who was calling, just by his or her voice—before the person on the other end told you who it was? Are you good at recognizing voices? *(Let kids respond.)* If we hear a voice that we've heard many times before, it's pretty easy to recognize, isn't it? *(You may share your own story here or ask kids to tell about a time when they recognized somebody by voice—without even seeing the person.)*

Do you know that a baby can recognize her mommy's voice when she is just a few days old? She's heard that voice from inside the mommy as she's growing and developing and getting ready to be born. Her mommy's voice is comforting and familiar. Sometimes just hearing the voice of her mother is enough to calm a crying baby.

People aren't the only ones who are good at recognizing voices. Plenty of animals are, too. Did you know that a flock of sheep can recognize the voice of their shepherd? Sheep aren't like dogs; you can't train them to do tricks. But sheep can recognize voices, and they can follow the familiar voice of their shepherd. When a flock of sheep is scared or confused, often just the sound of the shepherd's voice is enough to calm them and to bring them in close to the shepherd. The sheep don't have to see the shepherd; even in darkness, they will follow the sound of the shepherd's voice.

In the Bible, people are often compared to sheep and Jesus is called the Good Shepherd. What are some ways that

we can hear Jesus' voice talking to us? *(Let children share ideas.)* Do we hear his words in Bible readings? Do we hear what he wants us to know in the words of our parents and pastor and Sunday school teachers? And sometimes, do we hear Jesus' voice in the answers to our prayers?

A good shepherd is always looking for the safest path for his flock. He looks for green pastures with lots of tasty grass for his sheep. He takes his sheep to calm, clear water to drink. Jesus always wants the best for us, so we can feel very safe and happy when we follow his voice. Jesus said, "My sheep listen to my voice; I know them, and they follow me. I give them eternal life" (John 10:27-28 NIV). Jesus has promised his followers a wonderful life with him—one that will never end. And no one can take that away from us. Follow the Good Shepherd.

Dear Jesus, help us hear your voice, and then help us to follow that voice. Amen

Notes

Proving It to the World

Preparation: Bring along an example of a talent you possess or a special piece of art you've made or an unusual object that you own. For example, you could bring balls to juggle or a painting, a sculpture, or a piece of stitchery you've made.

Have any of you ever heard the expression, "The proof is in the pudding"? Let's say that your friend tells you he can make a pudding that is the best thing you have ever tasted. If you reply, "Well, the proof is in the pudding," you're saying that you'll believe him after you've tasted the pudding. In other words, if you're telling the truth about something, you will be able to show it.

(Describe your unusual talent or show your unusual passion here. My example follows.) I'd like to tell you about something I can do that I think is kind of special. I can juggle three balls at the same time. I suppose I could tell you that and not really know how to juggle, but you could always test me. You could say, "All right, prove it! The proof is in the pudding, you know." Then I would have to prove it to you. *(Pause for a bit, and if nobody challenges you, continue.)* "Well, is anyone going to say it to me?" *(Children can respond with "Prove it!")*

Okay then, I'll have to show you. I'll prove what I said was true. *(Demonstrate your talent or reveal your special possession to prove it's real.)* There. Now you see that what I said is true, right?

Jesus' followers were going around telling everyone that they were friends of Jesus—that they were his disciples. So

Jesus told those followers how to prove they really were—and the whole world would know they told the truth. Jesus told them that they should love one another the way Jesus loved them. Jesus said, "Your love for one another will prove to the world that you are my disciples" (John 13:35 NLT).

How do *we* prove to the whole world that we really are followers of Jesus? *(Let kids respond.)* We love each other. Instead of saying "the proof is in the pudding," we might say "the proof is in the loving." Is it hard to love sometimes? When your sister is making fun of you, is it hard to love her as much as Jesus loves her? When your brother has just eaten the last chocolate donut, is it hard to love him as much as Jesus loves him?

The love of Jesus is a powerful thing. Jesus loved us so much that he was willing to die for us on the cross. He wants us to love each other that much. And that love will show the world that we really are disciples of Jesus.

Dear Jesus, fill me up with your love so that I can love everyone else.

Notes

The Reminder

Preparation: Tie colored yarn around three of your fingers as visual reminders. You may cut extra lengths of yarn and bring these to hand out to children at the end of the sermon.

Why do you suppose I have these colored strings tied around my fingers? *(Hold your hand up and let children guess.)* Sometimes people tie strings around their fingers to remind them of something. Let's say you have to bring your turtle to school for show-and-tell. You want to be sure you don't forget, so you tie a string around your finger before you go to bed. In the morning, you see the string and remember to bring the turtle.

I don't have to remember anything for show-and-tell, but I do have to remember some important things every day. Would you like to know what my strings remind me of? *(Point to each string as you explain the following.)* This one reminds me that Jesus said, "You should love each other just as much as I love you." Another string reminds me that Jesus said, "Whenever you feed the hungry in my name, it's as if you are feeding me." Another string helps me remember that Jesus said, "Love your enemies and do good to those who hurt you." All of these strings remind me of important things Jesus said—things that I want to be sure to do.

The Gospel lesson from the book of John tells us about another way God reminds us of Jesus' words. Jesus told his disciples, "When the Father sends the Counselor . . . I mean the Holy Spirit . . . he will teach you everything and will remind you of everything I myself have told you" (NLT). So we don't really need strings, do we? We have God's Holy Spirit to help us remember Jesus' words.

I'll take these strings off now because I know the Holy Spirit will remind me of the things Jesus said. *(Remove strings as you give the following examples.)* If someone pushes you on the playground, the Holy Spirit might remind you that Jesus said we shouldn't be mean to those who are mean to us. Instead, we should treat them with love, and love can help change mean persons of this world. And if you see somebody who's poor and hungry, of what might the Holy Spirit remind you? *(Let children answer.)* Or, what if you see a classmate or friend who is lonely or sad? *(Let children answer.)*

The Holy Spirit will remind us of Jesus' words about loving one another, but we also have to remember to be good listeners and to listen for the Holy Spirit. So maybe I'll keep just one string to remind me to listen to the Holy Spirit. And maybe you might want a little reminder to listen, too. *(You may hand out strings to all the kids as reminders to listen.)*

Lord, help us to listen to your reminders, and help us to love as Jesus loves us.

Notes

Freedom for the Jailer

Preparation: Find or draw a large picture of a jailer standing outside a jail cell with a prisoner inside behind bars.

C an anyone tell me which of these two persons is in prison and which one is free? *(Hold up picture so children and congregation can see it. Let child point out the prisoner and the jailer.)* That was pretty easy to tell, wasn't it? Do you think the one who is outside the jail guarding the prisoner is always the one who is free? Let me tell you a true story about prisoners and a jailer. It's a story about two men who told many people about Jesus; their names were Paul and Silas.

This story is found in the New Testament book called Acts. Paul and Silas were thrown in prison by the people in a city whose ruler did not want them to preach about God. They were put in the inner dungeon, and their feet were clamped into irons so they couldn't even move. Their jailer was ordered to guard them carefully so they could not escape.

Now, it seems like the jailer is free and Paul and Silas are not free, doesn't it? But really, the opposite is true. Paul and Silas may have been in jail, but they didn't feel like prisoners. They were happy because they believed in Jesus and were free from the jail of sin. They were so happy about the freedom Jesus brings that they were singing at the top of their lungs, praising God. The jailer, on the other hand, didn't know Jesus, so he was still trapped in the prison of sin and bad thoughts.

Suddenly a great earthquake shook the jail from top to bottom! All the prison doors flew open, and the chains dropped off every prisoner. The jailer thought that all the prisoners had escaped, and he was really scared. He knew he would be punished for letting them escape, so he drew his sword and was about to kill himself. But Paul shouted, "Stop! We're all here!" The jailer ran to Paul and Silas and fell on his knees before them. These men seemed so happy, they sang hymns in prison; and they had been so kind to him—they hadn't even run away. He wanted to know how he, too, could be so happy and so kind. The jailer asked Paul and Silas, "Sirs, what must I do to be saved?"

Paul and Silas told the jailer, "Believe in the Lord Jesus Christ and you will be saved." So that very night the jailer and his whole family accepted Jesus as their Savior and were baptized.

Now the jailer was free from the prison of sin—just as free as Paul and Silas! And now he, too, could be happy and kind to others.

Lord Jesus, thank you for making us free from the power of sin.

Notes

The Language of God

Preparation (Optional): Arrange ahead of time for members of the congregation who are fluent in other languages to stand, one after the other and declare, "Jesus is Lord. I believe in Jesus!" in their various languages.

C an you tell me what language you speak? *(Let children respond.)* Many of us speak English, but in our country we hear other languages as well. Do any of you speak another language or know anyone who does? *(Let the children share. If some can do so, let them say a few words in another language. Or, if you know another language, say something to the children in that language.)* Does anyone know what language God speaks? *(Someone may answer.)*

When Jesus was preaching here on Earth, he spoke Aramaic, the language he learned as a little boy. Hebrew was the language that was used in the Jewish places of worship. And many of Jesus' early followers spoke Greek and Latin. So were those God's languages? The first followers of Jesus lived in the Middle East, so they spoke Middle Eastern languages when they told others about Jesus. Where can we find followers of Jesus today? *(Let kids respond.)* There are Christians in every country in the world now. The Bible is printed in more languages than any other book in the world!

Today we celebrate the Day of Pentecost, which is sort of like the birthday of the Christian Church. On this day, a lot of Jesus' followers were all together in one place. Jesus had gone back to be with his Father in heaven, but before he left,

he had told his disciples to wait for God's Spirit to come and show them what to do. Suddenly a sound like a mighty wind filled the room. Then, what looked like small flames appeared over the disciples' heads. Jesus' followers were filled with the Holy Spirit, and they began talking about Jesus in other languages. *(Ask volunteers to speak of Jesus in different languages.)*

(If you had volunteers speak in different languages, say: On that first Pentecost, it probably sounded a little like what you just heard.) The disciples began preaching in languages they had never known before. And there were people in the crowds who understood them. *And* the Holy Spirit knew those languages; the Holy Spirit helped them tell about Jesus.

How many languages do you think God knows? *(Children may answer.)* God can speak any language in the world to anyone in the world. And God speaks through followers just like us. You can each use the language you know in order to tell others about Jesus. The message of Jesus began to spread around the world on the first Pentecost, and it continues to spread whenever you tell others about Jesus.

Lord, give us the words to speak about you to people everywhere.

Notes

Strong Wind, Strong Branches

Preparation: Bring in a tree branch—preferably one that has fallen in a storm or been trimmed—to illustrate your talk.

I brought a tree branch with me this morning. *(Hold up branch and let children guess where it came from.)* After a big windstorm, you might find a lot of branches scattered around on the ground. Have any of you seen the mess that strong wind can make of leaves and branches? *(Kids can share some storm stories.)* If the wind is strong enough, it can break a big branch right off the tree—or even blow a whole tree over!

You know, from a tree's point of view, it might be better if there were no wind at all. Even ordinary wind can make things difficult for trees. The wind blows trees around and bends their branches this way and that, and sometimes breaks their branches.

Well, some years ago, scientists tried out an experiment with trees and wind. They built a huge, clear dome to enclose an area where animals and trees and other plants lived. Light could come in, but the space was closed off from the rest of the world in every other way. No air could enter from the outside, so there was no wind inside the dome.

At first the trees did very well. With no wind to bend or break their branches, the trees grew straight and tall; and after awhile some of the trees produced fruit. But as the fruit grew larger and heavier, the branches that held the fruit began to break! The trees were not strong enough to support their own fruit. The scientists discovered that trees need wind to build

strong branches. As wind pulls the tree and branches this way and that, they grow strong and flexible. Trees actually need the bothersome wind in order to grow strong!

People are a little bit like trees. We may not like it when bad things or troubles come our way. We may feel hurt if others tease us for believing in God and for always wanting to do things God's way. We may be pushed around by problems or by difficult people, but we don't have to be afraid. Those troubles can end up making us stronger if we keep trusting the Lord.

In the New Testament book of Romans, we learn that we can rejoice when we run into troubles, because they will make us strong inside. God will be with us in any and every trouble we face. And when we see how God helps us make it through one problem, we know God will be there for the next one, too—and the one after that.

And the more we see how God helps us, the more we trust in God.

Dear God, stay with us in every trouble and every bad thing we face. Show us how strong we can be when you are with us.

Notes

Mysterious Transformation

Preparation: Bring a chrysalis or pictures of cocoons and moths or butterflies. (A butterfly emerges from a chrysalis; a moth emerges from a cocoon.)

D o you know what a mystery is? Have you ever seen something mysterious? *(Let children respond.)* A mystery is something amazing, something very difficult or impossible to explain. *(Using the pictures or objects you brought with you, describe the transformation of an insect, such as caterpillar to butterfly. If possible, describe one you have seen yourself, or use my example below.)*

Here is a mystery I have seen. I have watched fat little caterpillars spin smooth, warm blankets around themselves. The caterpillars sleep inside those chrysalises, and many days later, something that is not at all like a caterpillar comes out. What does a caterpillar change into? *(Let children describe butterflies or moths they have seen emerge from these transformations.)* Yes! A caterpillar becomes a butterfly.

If you could see inside that tight covering, you'd find that the caterpillar doesn't look like it's alive. It's not moving; you can't see anything changing. It looks dead. Then one day, the chrysalis starts to shake and wobble. Slowly, an insect with wings pushes its way out into the world.

The chrysalis is a little bit like the tomb where Jesus was buried. When Jesus was laid in that tomb and the big stone was rolled in front of the entrance, everyone thought that was the last they'd see of Jesus. No one expected life to come out of that place of death. But after three days, God raised Jesus to new life. A transformed Jesus came out of that tomb, more alive than he had ever been before.

In 1 Corinthians, Paul writes, "But let me tell you a wonderful secret God has revealed to us. Not all of us will die, but we will all be transformed. It will happen in a moment, in the blinking of an eye. . . . Our . . . earthly bodies must be transformed into heavenly bodies that will never die" (15:51-53 NLT).

All of us are sort of like caterpillars. We know we're alive, but this is the only life we know. We walk along the ground like caterpillars crawl along a leaf. A little caterpillar can't imagine what it will be like to have wings and soar through the air. And like that caterpillar, we can't imagine what life will be like when we are living in heaven with our Savior. It's too wonderful to imagine. But Jesus has promised that we will have this special new life with him. We will be changed, transformed.

Dear Jesus, as we look forward to a new life with you in heaven, begin to change us now. Give us hearts that love you more and more, and hands that help others.

Notes

Impressing Jesus

Do you know what it means to "impress" someone? *(Let kids try to explain. Help them understand that this means to make someone think good things about us, to think we're special.)* What sorts of things might you do to impress your parents, for example? *(Let children give ideas.)* In order to impress you parents, you might clean up your whole room without even being asked. You might try really hard in school. If you practiced a musical instrument and enjoyed playing it, you would impress your parents. When someone is impressed by you, they admire you and are proud of what you did.

What might you do to impress your friends? *(Let children share their ideas.)* You might build a really cool fort and invite your friends over to play inside it. Perhaps you could create a really good painting in art, and your friends would admire it. Maybe you'd learn a new skateboard trick, and that would impress your friends.

Now, how do you think someone could impress Jesus? That's a tougher question to answer, isn't it? What would Jesus be most impressed by? *(Let children express their ideas.)* Would Jesus be impressed by someone who made a lot of money and had a huge house and lots of stuff? If someone designed a spaceship that carried astronauts all the way to Mars, would that impress Jesus? What if someone memorized the whole Bible from cover to cover; would that impress Jesus? Well, Jesus might be happy for people who could do these things, but none of these things would make Jesus think they were special people or make him love them more.

Today's Gospel reading tells about a man who really did impress Jesus. He was an officer in the Roman army who was respected by the Jews because he did many good things for them. One of the servants in this officer's house was very sick, and the officer cared very much for him. When the officer heard about Jesus, he sent a message to him. "I am not worthy to receive you in my house or even to come and meet you. Just say the word from where you are, and my servant will be healed" (Luke 7:6-7 NLT). When Jesus heard this, he was amazed. The Roman officer believed that Jesus was so powerful he could heal the sick servant just by speaking some words.

Jesus said, "I haven't seen faith like this in all the land of Israel!" (Luke 7:9 NLT). What impressed Jesus was the Roman officer's faith or trust in him. Faith—trusting God with all your heart and soul—that's what impresses Jesus.

Dear Jesus, give us faith that is as strong as that of the Roman officer.

Notes

Stronger than Death

Preparation: Bring a dead bug or butterfly mounted in a viewing box so children can observe it.

I brought a small creature with me this morning. If you handle the box very carefully, I'll pass it around so that you can get a closer look at it. *(Pass around dead bug in the box.)* Can anyone tell me what is inside the box? *(Let kids respond by describing the insect.)* Is the [bug] alive or dead? How can you tell that it's dead? *(Discuss.)* It's not moving, is it? It doesn't respond to anything. Sooner or later, do all things die? *(Talk about this.)* We'll die someday too, won't we? I hope we'll all be around to enjoy a good long life serving the Lord, but someday our bodies will stop working and we'll go to heaven to be with Jesus.

Is there any way that any of us could make this little bug live again? Can we bring this bug back to life? *(Let children comment.)* No, this isn't something anybody on Earth can do. We aren't stronger than death.

In reading the Bible, we learn about two sons who died. One son lived back in the time of Elijah the prophet, and the other lived while Jesus was walking around on Earth. Both of these boys were their mothers' only children. And both of the mothers were widows—their husbands had died. These mothers and sons had only each other in the world. When their sons died, the mothers had no one left. The pain of losing their only children was causing the mothers' hearts to break.

But God is the creator of life, and God is more powerful than death. And God loved these mothers very much. God had pity on the widow who was Elijah's friend. And God had pity on the widow from Nain who lived in Jesus' time. Maybe God was especially sad for them because God knew he would give his only Son up to die for the world.

God's power moved through the touch of Elijah and brought one widow's son back to life. Later, in the town of Nain, in the middle of a funeral procession, Jesus took the hand of the other widow's son, and the mighty power of God returned that boy to life. He sat up immediately and started to talk to the people around him.

Death is a powerful thing; it strikes every day. And it happens to all of us. But God's power is stronger than death. Because of Jesus, we will always live happily with God—even if our bodies die here on Earth.

Dear Jesus, thank you for giving us life with you that will never end.

Notes

The Weight of Sin

Preparation: Bring two objects for students to hold—one that is heavy (perhaps a thick book or telephone directory) and one that is fairly light (a small book or tablet).

I need two volunteers. You have to be strong enough to hold these weights while I'm talking. *(Choose two volunteers. Give one the heavy weight and the other the lighter weight. If the weights are not too heavy, have children hold them at arm's length to make it more difficult.)*

Jesus was once invited to an important man's home for a meal. Jesus had walked a long way, and he was tired and his feet were dusty. Back in those days, when someone special came to dinner, the host had a servant wash the guest's feet. Then the host would anoint the head of his guest with sweet-smelling oil. But when Jesus arrived, the important man did not have Jesus' feet washed, and he did not pour sweet-smelling oil on Jesus' head. After they sat down to eat, a woman came in with a jar of expensive perfume and poured it on Jesus' feet. Then she wiped his feet with her hair.

The important man was shocked! This woman was not someone he wanted to have in his house. She had done many bad and shameful things. He thought to himself: *This Jesus is not a great prophet like everyone says. If he were, he would know how bad this woman is, and he wouldn't let her touch his feet.* Jesus knew what the man was thinking, and he told a story that went something like this:

There were two people who were carrying heavy burdens.

One carried a burden weighing a hundred pounds, the other carried a burden weighing ten pounds. They could only let go of their burdens if someone else offered to take them. Both of the people were so tired. The one with the heavier weight didn't know if she could make it any longer. Suddenly someone offered to take their burdens. *(Take the weights from the volunteers and let them join the rest of the kids.)* Who do you suppose was more thankful: the one carrying the lighter weight or the one with the heavier weight? *(Let kids respond.)*

The woman who washed Jesus' feet was carrying a heavy weight of sin. She knew she had sinned a lot; she knew what other people thought about her. But she also knew that Jesus loved her and forgave her and took that weight of sin away. And the woman wanted to show Jesus how happy she was. The important man didn't think he had many sins. He thought he was much better than the woman. But he was wrong. All of us have sinned, and none of us is better than anybody else. Jesus forgives us all. And we should all be as thankful as that woman who washed Jesus' feet.

Jesus, thank you so very much for forgiving us and taking away the load of sin. We love you.

Notes

The Danger of Emptiness

Preparation: Bring a large balloon to inflate and enough balloons to hand out one to each child.

The Gospel lesson for today tells a story about a man who really needed Jesus' help. Jesus took a boat across a big lake. Jesus had barely stepped out of the boat when a wild man, dirty and ragged and scary looking, came running toward him. This man had no home. He had been living outside in a cemetery for a long time. People steered clear of this man because he frightened them. But this man was very unhappy, and he badly needed help.

When Jesus saw this man running toward him, he did not jump back in the boat or run away to safety. Jesus knew how to help the man. You see, there were evil spirits—sent by the devil—who were making the man wild and crazy. They threw the man about and made him run into the wilderness. Jesus knew that God was much more powerful than these evil spirits or the devil. Jesus commanded the evil spirits to come out of the man. As soon as the evil spirits left the man, he was normal. He got dressed and sat quietly at Jesus' feet. From that day on, he told everyone about the wonderful love and power of Jesus who had saved him.

How did those evil spirits get into that man in the first place? (*Let kids respond. The evil spirits are agents of the devil.*) How was the man different after Jesus helped him? (*Again let kids discuss. The evil spirits had left him. He was calm. He loved Jesus.*) After Jesus healed the man, God's love and faith in Jesus filled him. Do you think it would be easy for those evil spirits to come back into him now? *(Let children answer.)*

Can you pour something bad, like poison, into an empty container? *(Let kids respond.)* Yes, you can. But what if a container is full, already packed with something good? Could you pour poison into a full container? No, you can't. Nothing else will fit.

We are sort of like this balloon. If we are empty, anything can be poured into us. *(Hold up limp balloon.)* This balloon could be filled with water or gasoline or dirt or even poison. But if God's love fills us, there isn't room for evil things to enter in. *(Blow up balloon and hold end closed.)* We can keep this air in the balloon or release it. In the same way, we can accept and welcome God's Spirit in our lives, or we can reject him. But God wants to fill us up with his love; he wants to fill us up with good things so that no evil can enter us. *(Tie your balloon off at this point.)* Each of you can take a balloon to remind you to let God fill you up with his Spirit. *(Hand out a balloon to each child.)*

Lord, fill us with faith in you. Fill us with your love and your life so that we won't have any room for evil inside.

Notes

Don't Look Back

Preparation: Make a long straight line with tape on the floor near where you meet with the children—for example, from the steps of the altar partway down the center aisle.

If Jesus came into church right now and asked you to follow him, what would you do? *(Let children answer.)* Now, what if Jesus told you that if you follow him, you will be sleeping out in the rain in cardboard boxes? Would it be easy to follow him? *(Let children answer.)* What if Jesus said, "I want you to come and be my disciple right now. There isn't time to run back and say good-bye to your family." Would it be hard to follow Jesus then? *(Discuss.)* Of course, kids always have to tell their parents where they're going. But if you were grown up, this could be a choice you would have to make.

Jesus was on his way to the city of Jerusalem, and he knew he was going to die on a cross. On his way, Jesus invited some grown-ups to come along with him; and some other people asked if they could go with Jesus. Not all of them ended up going with Jesus, however, because they had to make tough choices. Some of the people said they would follow Jesus, but first they had to take care of important matters, or first they had to say good-bye to their families. Jesus told them, "No one who puts his hand to the plow and looks back is fit for service in the kingdom of God" (Luke 9:62 NIV).

Have you ever tried to draw a long straight line on the sidewalk with chalk? It's easy to end up with a wobbly line, isn't it? Well, it's even harder to cut a straight line in the soil with a plow. The person plowing has to use a big blade that cuts the soil. He has to keep his eyes straight ahead to see where he is going, and he has to concentrate really hard. If he keeps turning around to look behind him, what do you think will happen to the line in the dirt? (*Let kids answer.*)

I'd like two volunteers to help me out. (*Choose volunteers.*) I want you to take turns walking down this line. [Name of Child One], you will keep your eyes straight ahead, watching carefully where you're going. Don't look around, even if you hear us yell, "Hey!" (*Try this with first volunteer.*) [Name of Child Two], you will walk straight down the line, but when you hear us yell, turn your head and look at us while you walk. (*Try this with second volunteer.*) Who did a better job of walking a straight line? (*Discuss.*)

It's not always easy to follow Jesus. But it always helps to keep our eyes on him, to watch and pray so we see where he wants us to go. When we take our eyes off Jesus, when we forget about him, that's when our lives start to go crooked.

Jesus, we want to follow you. Help us keep our eyes on you and go where you lead us.

Notes

You Reap What You Sow

Preparation: Bring several packets of seeds and, if possible, a dried weed with the seeds intact.

Can anyone tell me what I'm holding here? *(Show packets of seeds and let kids respond. Adapt the following examples to the kinds of seeds you brought to show.)* These are seeds, aren't they? If I wanted [sunflowers] to grow in my front yard, which packet of seeds would I plant or sow? "To sow" is another way of saying "to plant." *(Kids can choose appropriate packet.)* If I wanted [red, juicy tomatoes] to grow, which packet of seeds would I sow? *(Let kids respond.)* Yes! If I sow tomato seeds in my garden, after awhile I will be able to reap ripe tomatoes. "To reap" is another way of saying "to gather" or "to pick." We all know that in order to get a certain kind of plant to grow we have to sow the right kind of seed.

Here I have a weed. *(Show weed.)* This is the type of weed that could take over a garden and choke out all the other plants. What would happen if I sowed these weed seeds in my garden? Would I get anything good to eat or pretty to look at? *(Children may answer.)* No. I would just get weeds.

In the book of Galatians, the Bible says, "Don't be misled. Remember that you can't always ignore God and get away with it. You will always reap what you sow!" Every day, each one of you is planting seeds—some are good and some are bad. The things you plant will either help to make you a better person or a worse person. I'll tell you what kinds of seeds I'm talking about.

Let's say you wake up in a grumpy mood and instead of trying to be happy and treat others well, you decide to stay grumpy. And before you know it, your grumpiness turns into anger, and you end up calling your sister or brother a bad name. Is that a good seed that you planted or a bad seed? *(Let kids respond.)* What you reap from that bad seed will be bad feelings and unhappiness, and maybe a punch or a shove in return. That's a bad weed from a bad seed.

Or maybe you wake up in a bad mood, but instead of staying grumpy, you close your eyes and pray to Jesus to take the grumpiness away. And then you try to think of something good and kind, and you give somebody in your family a big hug. Is that a good seed you just planted or a bad seed? *(Let kids respond.)* Because you made a good choice and asked God to help you do the right thing, you will probably reap something good in return—maybe a hug back. Something good comes from a good seed.

Dear Jesus, help us always to plant good seeds; help us to turn bad thoughts, feelings, and behaviors into good and kind ones.

Notes

Who Is Your Neighbor?

Once upon a time, Jesus was teaching about being kind and loving to one's neighbors. One of the men listening asked Jesus, "Who is my neighbor?" The man wanted to know who he had to be kind and loving to. And to answer him, Jesus told a story.

I'd like to tell you a story that's a little bit like the story Jesus told. Do you remember that man's question? *(Let kids answer: "Who is my neighbor?")* See if you can find the answer to that question in my story. While you're listening, if you like, you may hold hands with one of your friends.

One day, not too long ago at a school near here, a little boy was swinging on the monkey bars in the far corner of the playground. Because it had just rained and the bars were slippery, the boy lost his grip, hit his lip on the metal bar, twisted his leg badly, and fell smack into the middle of a mud puddle. The boy was bleeding and hurt. He couldn't stand up by himself, and he was very dirty. He couldn't cry very loudly because his ribs hurt when he took a breath.

The prettiest girl in his class walked by on her way to the water fountain. Her hair was always neatly brushed and her socks were never dirty. She saw the boy lying there in the puddle and could see that he was hurt, but she didn't want to stop and help. "I might get mud on my lace socks," she thought. "And I might get blood stains on my beautiful dress." "And besides, I'm not really friends with that boy." So she walked by him, got her drink of water, and ran off to play.

The next child to see the hurt boy was in a big hurry. He was playing lightning tag, and he had only a few seconds to tag two more people and win. This boy was proud of being the fastest kid in his class. He was also very strong and could easily have picked the muddy boy up and given him a piggy-back ride to the nurse's office. But he wanted to win the game, so he ran right past the boy with barely a glance.

Finally, along came a small girl who wasn't even in the same class as the boy. She heard the boy crying softly and walked closer to see what was the matter. This girl was not very popular, she didn't have many friends, and she was very shy. It took a lot of courage for her to walk up to that boy and ask him if he needed help. When he nodded his head, she walked right into the mud puddle, helped him up, and, even though she wasn't very strong, helped him limp to the nurse's office. And then she even helped bandage him up.

Now I'd like to ask you: which kid was a good neighbor to the hurt boy? *(Let children respond.)* Our friends are our neighbors, and so are the people who live near us. But Jesus wants us to be good neighbors to *anyone* who needs our help and friendship—even those people we don't usually play with.

Jesus, make us all good neighbors; help us show your love to everyone who needs your love.

Notes

Distracting Details

How do your families get ready for church? What sort of things do you do in the morning so that everyone is ready to go to church? *(Let children share their stories.)* Most of us eat breakfast in the morning, brush our teeth, and comb our hair. Some will find nice, new clothes to wear. Some women may put on makeup and fix their hair. Some men may wear a tie or even polish their shoes. And, most important of all, some families say a prayer asking God to help them listen and learn in church. We can honor God by the way we get ready to worship on Sundays.

What if we went through all the motions of getting ready to go to church on a Sunday morning, but we never got out the door? What if we were so busy getting ready and making sure we looked just right and had the perfect outfit on, that we never made it to church? Would we have missed the most important thing? *(Let kids respond.)* Why do we come to church on Sunday? *(Let kids discuss.)* Is it just so we can get dressed up and see our friends? Sunday worship is for praising God and thanking God and joining with other Christians in prayer and singing. We go to hear about Jesus and to listen to his words read from the Bible.

Today's Gospel lesson from the book of Luke tells about a time when Jesus went to visit some friends named Mary and Martha. Martha welcomed Jesus into her home and then went scurrying about cleaning the house and getting lots of food prepared for a big feast that they were having in Jesus' honor. Her sister, Mary, on the other hand, sat down at Jesus' feet and listened to Jesus as he taught her.

Martha did not think that Mary was being fair by not helping her. So she said to Jesus, "Lord, doesn't it seem unfair to you that my sister just sits here while I do all the work? Tell her to come and help me." But Jesus replied, "My dear Martha, you are so upset over all these details! There is really only one thing you need to be concerned about. Mary has discovered it—and I won't take it away from her."

Having Jesus come to your house and then not even taking time to listen to him is like getting all ready for church and then not going to church. Even if we do come to church, sometimes we start thinking about all kinds of things that take our mind off Jesus, and we may forget to listen to what Jesus is trying to teach us. For the rest of the worship service today, I want you to try hard to keep your mind on Jesus. When you join in the songs and prayers and really listen to the sermon, it's like sitting at the feet of Jesus and listening to what he has to teach you!

Dear Jesus, teach us to listen to you with all our heart.

Notes

God's Good Gifts

Preparation: Hollow out the inside of a delicious-looking cupcake or roll and fill it with dirt or another inedible substance. Bring a cutting board and a butter knife.

Can you think of some really good things that you might ask your parents for? *(Let children share their ideas.)* Your parents give you lots of good things, don't they? But what are some things you ask for that might not be so good for you? *(Again let children list things.)* If we asked our folks to let us stay up all night on a school night and watch movies, do you think they would let us? Our parents want to make sure we get rest so we stay healthy and happy and strong. How about if we asked our parents for a nice, juicy apple? Do you think they would give that to us? Of course. They would like us to have a good, healthy snack.

When Jesus was teaching his disciples about prayer, he said, "You fathers—if your children ask for a fish—do you give them a snake instead? Or if they ask for an egg, do you give them a scorpion? Or course not! If you sinful people know how to give good gifts to your children, how much more will your heavenly Father give the Holy Spirit to those who ask him" (Luke 11:11-13 NLT). God wants to give us good things even more than parents want to give their kids good things.

If we ask God for something that really, truly is good for us, God will give it to us. What if we ask for something that *we* think is good for us, but God knows it would hurt us? *(Let kids respond.)* What if we asked God for a million dollars, but

God knew it would make us greedy and unhappy; would God give that to us? No, God wants us to be happy and to love him more than things or money.

I have a delicious-looking [cupcake] here. Would anyone want to ask me for a bite of it? *(Let kids respond.)* You may think you want this [cupcake]; it looks good, doesn't it? But I'm not going to give you a piece. I know something that you don't. Let me cut the [cupcake] open so you can see what's inside. *(Cut the cupcake open on the cutting board to reveal the inedible insides.)* Do you see why I didn't give you what you asked for? God wants us to pray to him whenever we want anything, but we have to remember to trust that God knows what is best and will give us only things that would be good for us.

Dear heavenly Father, thank you for being our good parent and for giving us everything we need.

Notes

Saving Up Bubbles

Preparation: Bring a bottle of bubble liquid, a bubble-blowing wand, and a large opaque bag, such as a black garbage bag.

I brought a bottle of bubble mix with me this morning. *(Hold up the bottle of bubble liquid and the wand so kids can see them.)* I want to blow lots of bubbles, and I want to keep them all for myself. I brought a big bag to keep them in. *(Start blowing bubbles into bag.)* See all my bubbles? They're all mine. I'm rich! And after I fill this bag with bubbles, I'll get more and more bags and save more and more bubbles for myself. I'll be the richest bubble owner in the world. *(Blow more bubbles into bag, then squeeze it shut.)*

Would you like to see all the bubbles I've saved? *(Open bag to show kids without looking yourself.)* Can you count all my bubbles? So many that you can't even count them, right? *(Children will observe that the bag is empty.)* What! Where did all my precious bubbles go? Did you take them? Did someone steal my bubbles? *(Let kids respond.)* They popped? You mean I blew all those bubbles for nothing? All my riches are gone. I just as well could have shared my bubbles with you, then, I guess. Then we all could have enjoyed them.

You know, this all reminds me of a parable that Jesus once told. He wanted to teach a lesson to a couple of brothers who were fighting over money. In Jesus' story, there was a rich man who had lots and lots of grain from his farm—so much grain that he couldn't fit it into his barns. He decided to tear down his barns and build bigger ones. He didn't think to share his riches. He wanted to save it only for himself. But this story turned out a little like my bubble collection. Just when the rich man had stored up more and more grain, he suddenly died. All that grain—all those riches—didn't do him any good at all. He couldn't take the riches with him.

Do you think that man would have been happier if he had shared his food and riches with people around him? What else might he have done with all his riches? *(Let kids answer.)* He could have made a lot of people happy. He could have made God happy. All of us have riches and special things we can share with others. What are some things we can share? *(Let kids answer.)* We can share our toys and our money. We can do good things for each other and help our neighbors. We can even share our smiles and our friendship.

You know, I would have much more fun sharing my bubbles with all of you rather than trying to save them in a bag. *(Blow some bubbles.)* God gives us good gifts so we can share them with others. Thanks for sharing my bubbles with me before they disappeared.

Lord, teach us to share the riches that you give us.

Notes

Ready for the Knock

Preparation: Bring small birthday candles to hand out. Arrange for someone to knock loudly on a door when you give the signal (to the pastor's office, to the sacristy, anywhere where the children will be able to hear it during the sermon).

I'd like to read part of today's Gospel reading to you. It's from Luke, chapter 12: "Let your loins be girded and your lamps burning, and be like men who are waiting for their master to come home from the marriage feast, so that they may open to him at once when he comes and knocks" (vv. 35-36 RSV). Do you know what that means? First of all, "Let your loins be girded" means to get your long robes out of the way—to put a belt around them to hold them up so that you can run fast. To us today, this would mean to get dressed and be ready to go somewhere at a minute's notice. Second, "let your lamps be burning" means something, too. In Jesus' day, people used oil lamps that had a flame, sort of like a candle. The lamps should be ready to give light so the people can see to go outside in the dark. Then the Bible says to be like people who are waiting for someone special to arrive. In other words, Jesus is telling his listeners to be all ready to go and to wait for that special person—the master—to come.

Who do you think this verse is talking about? Who is the Master that we should all get ready for? *(Let children respond.)* These verses are talking about Jesus. He's coming back someday to take us all with him to heaven. Does anyone know the exact day or time when he will return? *(Someone may offer an answer.)* Nobody knows for sure. The Bible just tells us always to be ready. How can we be ready for Jesus to come again? What kinds of things should we be doing? *(Listen to responses.)* Helping our parents, praying, sharing, learning about God, singing praises, telling others about Jesus.

If Jesus suddenly showed up at your house and knocked on your door, what would you do? You'd jump up and open the door, right? Well, I brought some tiny lamps with me today. These little candles can be our lamps—even though they're not lit—and we'll pretend that we're waiting for Jesus to knock on that door. *(Point to nearby door.)* I want everyone to hold onto your candles and close your eyes. When you hear a knock, open your eyes, run to the door, and pretend to let Jesus in. Let's try it. *(Give signal for knock. Let children run to open the door.)*

Good. It looked like all of you were ready. I know we'll also be ready when Jesus really does return. Thanks for coming up this morning. You can all take your candles and go back to your seats now.

Jesus, keep us always ready for the happy time when you come back.

Notes

Throw Off the Weights

How many of you have ever run in a race? *(Let kids respond.)* If we were going to have to run in a long race, what things could we do to get ready? *(Discuss children's ideas.)* We could get in shape by practicing. We could eat healthy things before the race so we'd have energy. We could wear lightweight clothes and good, sturdy shoes. And let's all stretch our muscles like we're getting ready to run in a race. *(Stretch out with kids.)*

Now this is going to be a walking race (no running in church, you know), and it's going to be for just one racer—so I'd like one volunteer to be my fast walker. The rest of us will be the cheering crowd. *(Pick a volunteer—an older child who is fairly tall.)* Let's put our walker in the middle aisle, and the race will be from the front of the church to the back. The fast walker has to wait until I say go, and then we can all cheer him or her on. But before the race starts, I'm going to add something to make our walker's race more difficult. Can I have a few more volunteers? *(Choose four or six more children and have them sit on walker's feet and hold onto walker's legs.)* Now *(to the racer)*, because you have some kids on your feet, you have to be careful not to hurt them. But still try to get to the back of the church. On your mark, get set, go! *(Cheer as walker tries to go a few steps, then stop the race.)*

You can't race like this, can you? There's too much weight slowing you down. Let's remove these weights from your feet and legs and let you try again. But first, listen while I read a couple of verses from Hebrews, chapter 12.

"Therefore, since we are surrounded by such a huge crowd of witnesses to the life of faith, let us strip off every

weight that slows us down, especially the sin that so easily hinders our progress. And let us run with endurance the race that God has set before us" (v. 1 NLT).

All of us are in the race God has set before us—our lives are like a race. We try to do what God wants us to do as we walk through life. If we're carrying around sin and anger and bad feelings, those things can slow us down just like the kids slowed down our racer. We can pray for God's help to keep us from sin and anger and bad feelings, and we can let God's forgiveness take away the weight of the sins we do commit. When we've finished the race and come to the end of our lives, what happens? *(Let children answer.)* Jesus is waiting for us, isn't he? And the people who have gone on before us to heaven are there to cheer us on and encourage us to keep going.

Lord Jesus, take away all sins and bad things that slow us down and keep us from running toward you.

Now let's try that walking race once more, and let's all cheer our racer on! *(Start walker again. After race, let kids walk quickly back to their places.)*

Notes

Hands for Healing

Preparation: Bring heart-shaped stickers to hand out or a heart-shaped stamp and ink pad.

Good morning! I'd like everyone to raise your hands. Good! I see lots of hands in the air. Now put your hands down and look at them carefully. Really carefully. Your hands are very special. What can those hands do? Tell us some of the good things that you can do with your hands. (*Let children describe different activities.*) Our hands can tie shoelaces, plant seeds, pet kitty cats, write, and draw. Our hands can do so many good things.

Are hands able to do bad things, too? (*Kids may respond.*) What are some things that hands can do that are not so good? (*Children can give examples.*) It's too bad that hands can be used for hitting or pushing people away or writing things that are mean.

Jesus knows how special and wonderful hands are, and he used his hands to do amazing things. The Gospel lesson for today talks about a wonderful thing that Jesus did with his hands. A woman came to see Jesus. The woman was all bent over and could not straighten up; she had been that way for eighteen years. And do you know what Jesus did with his hands? He put his hands on the woman and healed her. She straightened up right away, and she said, "Praise God! Thank you for healing me!"

Jesus often used his hands for healing. He knew how to use his hands to help people and to love people. I want to

give each of you something to remind you today to use your hands in a loving way. *(Place heart sticker or heart stamp on each child's hand.)*

When you see this heart on your hand, remember how Jesus used His hands to heal people; remember how Jesus used his hands to help and comfort and touch those around him. Be thankful for your hands and use them like Jesus did.

Take our hands, Lord Jesus, and use them to do good, kind things for others.

Notes

Give It Away

Preparation: Bring pennies to hand out to each child.

C an anyone tell me something that you *really* love? What do you love? *(Let children offer responses.)* Name the people in your life whom you love. *(Kids answer.)* Because you love those people, how do you act toward them, and what do you do for them? *(Discuss with children.)* It's good to love people isn't it? God blesses us with many wonderful people to love.

I have here a penny. This is my penny. And I have one penny for each of you. *(Hold out other pennies and hand one to each child.)* Now if I told you that I really loved this penny, and that I had a special place for it to sit at my house, and that I held my penny every day and sang to it and kissed it, what would you think about that? *(Kids may respond.)* That would be pretty weird, wouldn't it? I shouldn't be spending my love on a penny.

This morning's Bible reading from Hebrews talks about that sort of foolish love: "Keep your lives free from love of money, and be content with what you have; for [God] has said, 'I will never leave you or forsake you'" (Heb. 13:5 NRSV). And it also says, "Do not neglect to do good and to share what you have, for such sacrifices are pleasing to God" (v. 16 NRSV).

In other words, the Bible says, "Don't love money," and "Share what you have." Do you think that's hard to do sometimes? *(Let children talk about times when it was hard to share*

something they had.) It can be hard to share, especially if you only have one of something—like one penny or one dollar or one best friend, can't it?

But do you know what? When we love Jesus and when we love other people so much that we want to share just to make them happy—*we* feel happier, too. And we feel richer than we did before!

You can go back to your seats now, but I want you to do something that might be difficult. On your way back to your seat, give your penny to someone else. Give that penny away, and I know that you will get lots of smiles in return. And then see if you don't feel better!

Jesus, help us to love you most of all, and help us to share what you have given us with people whom we love and you love.

Notes

Count the Cost

Preparation: Make two large signs—one reading, "LIFE" and the other, "DEATH."

Think of a toy that you *really* would like to have. *(Let kids respond.)* Let's pretend that your parents say you can have it if you pay for it. So you start saving. You save up money from your allowance. You save your gift money. You work at jobs on the weekends and save all of that money, too. Finally, after a whole year, you have enough money to buy the toy. You walk into the toy store, and you look at the toy once more before you buy it. Then you look at the money in your hand, and you think about how long it took to earn that money and how much work you did and how many dollars you put aside. Suddenly a thought enters your head: *It's not worth it. This toy is not worth it.* And so you take your hard-earned money and walk out of the store.

Before you make a big decision, it is important to count the cost. You have to ask, "How much is it worth to me?" Before we decide to follow Jesus with our whole hearts, God wants us to think about our decision very carefully. In the Old Testament reading, God told the Israelites that they had a really important decision to make: they could either follow the one true God or else follow the old, pretend gods. Choose God and life, or choose the pretend gods and death. *(Let two kids hold the signs you made, one on either side of you.)* Life or Death. It seems like an easy decision, doesn't it?

Point to which one you would choose. *(Let kids point to "LIFE.")* That was easy, but sometimes it's not such an easy choice to follow God. If some of your friends are using God's name in a careless way, or if they think that going to church is silly, it may be hard to tell them that Jesus is the most important thing in your life and you want to do what he wants you to. If all of your friends are going to see a movie that you know Jesus wouldn't want you to see, it may be hard to tell them why you aren't going with them. If your friends want you to join them in teasing another kid in your class, it might be hard to stand up to them and tell them to stop it. Following Jesus is not always easy.

The decision to follow Jesus is the most important choice you will make in your whole life. Even though it may be hard at times to be a Christian, it is always worth it. And Jesus has promised to be with us all the time and to help us. I hope all of you will choose to follow Jesus. He will give you life and all of the blessings that come with it.

Dear Jesus, help me to make the best and wisest decision; help me to follow you—always.

Notes

Find the Sheep!

Preparation: Before the service hide a stuffed toy sheep somewhere in the sanctuary not too far from where you meet with the kids. It shouldn't be too difficult for children to find.

Good morning! How are you this morning? (*Let children respond.*) Say, have any of you ever lost something that meant a lot to you? How does that feel? (*Let kids share several experiences of loss and the feelings they had.*) If you search and search and finally find what you had lost, how do you feel then? (*Kids respond.*) Well, I'm feeling sad this morning because I'm missing a sheep. I can't find my special little sheep. I brought her to church with me this morning, but she got away from me and disappeared. I'm pretty sure she's somewhere in this room.

I feel a little bit like the shepherd in this morning's Gospel lesson from Luke. This lesson tells about a shepherd who has one hundred sheep, and if he's missing one, he will go and look and look for that sheep until he finds it. Every single sheep is very important to a good shepherd. Will you help me find my sheep? We'll all look for her, and then when we find her, we'll celebrate, okay?

(*Let children spread out throughout the sanctuary and look for the sheep; when they find it, have everyone gather up front once more.*) Hurrah! We found the lost sheep. I am so happy. Do you know that Jesus is like that shepherd who went looking for the one lost sheep? Jesus wants everyone in the world to be a part of his flock. He wants everyone to know God's love.

It's wonderful that some of us grow up in God's family and have always known that God loves us. But there are lots of lost sheep out there, a lot of people who don't know Jesus. And Jesus is looking for those lost sheep. He wants to rescue those sheep.

When we tell people about God and treat them with kindness and invite them to church, we are helping Jesus find his lost sheep. And do you know what happens when Jesus finds a lost sheep? There's a big party in heaven—a celebration! Luke 15:10 says, "I tell you, there is joy in the presence of the angels of God over one sinner who repents" (NRSV).

So now you know how to start a party in heaven: teach someone that Jesus loves them. I hope all of you get to start many heavenly parties!

Lord Jesus, thank you for being our Good Shepherd. Help us always to be on the lookout for lost sheep to bring to you.

Notes

Choose Your Train

Preparation: Bring two toy trains or two pictures of train engines to illustrate your sermon.

H ow many of you have ever ridden on a train or seen a train going down the track? *(Let kids respond.)* Once a train is going in one direction, it's hard to turn that train around and make it go in another direction. Why do you think that's true? *(Discuss.)* A train runs on a track, and once it has started out in a certain direction, it usually continues in that direction. It's even hard to slow a train down once it picks up speed.

Let's pretend we're all standing on the platform at a train station. We're getting ready to take a trip and there are two trains waiting at the station. One train is brand new and very fancy. It is painted with gold and silver paint and the seats are red velvet. The dining car is full of delicious food from the fanciest restaurants. The sleeping car has feather beds with satin sheets. This train has a big sign on it that reads, "MONEY." In order to ride this train, you don't have to have lots of money; you just have to agree that money is more important than anything in the world.

The other train waiting at the station is going in the exact opposite direction. It is an older train, very plain looking. It hasn't been painted for quite some time. The seats are made of wood and they don't look very comfortable. The dining car has enough food—healthy, good food—but it's not at all fancy. The sleeping car is small with few beds, and people have to take turns sleeping and sitting. The beds have thin

  *Scolding the Snakes*

mattresses and blankets that are warm but very plain. This train has a large sign hanging on it too. In large, plain letters, the sign reads, "GOD." In order to ride this train, you don't have to be rich or poor, but you have to believe that God is the most important thing in life and that money is supposed to be used to help others.

As we look around, we see that lots of people are boarding the fancy train and laughing at the few people who decide to ride the plain train. You just happen to notice a large map hanging on the wall of the station that clearly shows where each train is going to end up. You notice that the "Money" train goes along an easy, flat track, then heads downhill. The track disappears at the end of a cliff. The "God" train heads up into the mountains into rugged land but ends at a beautiful place marked, "Heaven."

You look at both trains once again. And then in your imagination you get on a train. Sometime today I want you to tell someone which train you chose to get on and why you picked the train you did.

Jesus, help us all to make the right choices in our lives; and let us help others with the choices they must make.

Notes

Rich or Poor?

Preparation: If you feel comfortable doing so, bring two dolls to serve as Lazarus and the rich man, and practice moving them like puppets as you retell Jesus' parable. It would be good to practice several times before presenting the story.

How many of you would like to be really rich when you grow up? Can you tell me why? *(Children can respond.)* How many of you would not mind being poor? Raise your hands. The Gospel for this morning was a story Jesus told about a poor man named Lazarus and a rich man. *(Hold up the two dolls.)* We'll pretend that this doll is the rich man and this doll is the poor man, and I'll tell the story in a modern setting.

(As you tell the following story, move the dolls to "act out" the things you describe.) There was a rich man who loved to shop at the mall, and he always looked very spiffy. He spent lots of money on himself. He had a huge house and a four-car garage all to himself. At his gate, lying in the street, was a poor, sick, and very thin man named Lazarus. The poor man just wanted a few scraps of leftovers from the rich man's table, but the rich man wouldn't give him anything. Soon poor Lazarus died, and he was carried to heaven by angels to be with God. The rich man died, too, and he went to hell, where he was not at all happy.

It was a sad ending for the rich man but a happy ending for the poor man. Do you think Jesus wants us to think it's bad to be rich? *(Let children answer.)* Some people think the

Bible says that money is the root of all evil, but it doesn't say that. It says that the *love of money* is the root of all kinds of evil. It is hard to love God if riches are very, very important to you, because the money and things you can buy take up so much of your love. Can you take your toys or clothes or cars with you to heaven? *(Kids respond.)* In the end, those things aren't very important, are they? It's more important to be with God.

So how could you be rich and serve God at the same time? *(Children may answer.)* You can serve God by using your money for doing good in the world. You can share your food and toys with others. You can give much of the money that you make back to God. All good gifts come from God. When we bring our offerings to church, we're giving back to God a small part of what already belongs to God.

All good things come from you, heavenly Father. Help us to share the good things we have with others and to give them back to you.

Notes

Mustard Seed Faith

Preparation: Bring a packet of small seeds, a little pot of dirt, and, if possible, some small sprouts growing in a pot.

Sometimes it seems really hard to have faith in God. We can't see God; we can't hear God answering our questions or our prayers. At times we might wonder if we even have much faith at all. Jesus' own disciples felt the same way sometimes. They had Jesus right there with them, but still they felt like they didn't have enough faith.

One day the disciples said to Jesus, "We need more faith. Tell us how to get it." Jesus didn't really give them a direct answer. He didn't say, "Go down the street to the health food store and you can pick up a pound of faith there." But he did give them an answer—even though it seems a little hard to understand. He said, "Even if you had faith as small as a mustard seed, you could say to this mulberry tree, 'May God uproot you and throw you into the sea,' and it would obey you!" (Luke 17:6 NLT).

A mustard seed is very small. I have some seeds here that are about the same size as a mustard seed. (*Distribute seeds so kids can examine them.*) Do you think you might have faith at least as big as a mustard seed? That doesn't seem like a lot of faith, does it? Will these seeds ever amount to anything? If we just hold the seeds in our hands and never plant them, the seeds definitely will never get any bigger.

What would happen if we planted these seeds? (*Let children answer.*) The seeds would sprout and grow into plants

that are much bigger than the seeds. A huge tree can grow from a tiny seed.

Maybe Jesus was trying to get his disciples to see that it really wasn't their faith that was so powerful; it was what God could do with that faith. God could do amazing things with their lives when they put their trust in him. Just as you have to put the seed in the soil for it to grow, you have to actually put your faith in God for your faith to grow. If we put our faith in our friends, would that work just as well? *(Let kids respond.)* No, that would be sort of like trying to plant our seed in a pot of yogurt or peanut butter. We have to plant our faith seed in good soil. Our faith must be planted and rooted in God. He will grow our faith for us. And then we can do all kinds of wonderful things through God's power.

Lord, help us put our faith in you, and then make it grow and grow!

Notes

Erasing the Mark

thank you not

Preparation: Bring a stamp and stamp pad.

H ave any of you had chicken pox? Raise your hand if you've already had chicken pox. Did you enjoy having chicken pox? Did other people have to stay away from you while you were sick? How did you look? *(Let children offer responses and stories.)* Having chicken pox wasn't much fun, was it?

The Bible readings for today talk about people who had a disease called leprosy. Leprosy is not something anyone would ever want to catch. It's much more serious than chicken pox. It didn't just go away. In biblical times, when someone had leprosy, it never went away. People that had leprosy were called lepers, and others never wanted to go near them because they were afraid of catching the disease. Lepers were not very pleasant to look at. Sometimes their skin would be all lumpy and peeling; they might be missing toes or noses. These were like signs or marks that told people, "I'm sick," and when people saw those signs, they stayed far away.

Do you think lepers had many friends? How do you think they must have felt? *(Let kids share.)* Even though most people would not go near lepers, Jesus was different. Jesus could see that the lepers needed love and healing just like everyone else. Jesus talked to lepers, touched them, and healed them. And when Jesus healed people with leprosy, the disease was completely erased; they were well again!

Scolding the Snakes

None of us has leprosy, but when we do bad things, it's like having leprosy inside. We know we've done wrong, and we feel ugly inside. We feel bad, and we feel like everyone is staring at us, like nobody loves us or wants to be around us. Have you ever felt that way after you did something wrong? *(Let children respond.)* Now even though no one would be able to tell from the outside that we've done something wrong, Jesus knows. And when we've sinned, and we ask Jesus for help, what does he do for us? He forgives us and washes away our sins completely. He heals us and makes us clean inside.

(Begin stamping ink marks on children's hands as you speak.) I brought a stamp pad this morning, and I'll give each of you a mark to remind you of the people with leprosy that Jesus healed. This will remind you, too, of how Jesus heals us by forgiving our sins. Keep the mark on your hand till the end of the service, and later, when you wash your hands, remember that Jesus washes away our sins.

Jesus, thank you for washing away my sins and making me healthy and whole.

Notes

Truth vs. Myth

Preparation: Bring some book collections of your favorite fairy tales, fables, and myths (about Greek or Nordic gods, for example); also bring a Bible.

How many of you like to hear stories? Do you like to hear fairy tales or adventure stories read to you? What are some of your favorite stories? *(Let children share.)* I love stories too. I brought along some of my favorite stories from when I was young. *(Show the book collections and talk briefly about a few of your favorite stories.)* Some of these stories are called myths. A myth is a story that people have made up to explain how something came into being. There are many myths from different lands, for example, about how the world was made or how different creatures were made.

(You may share some myths that you have heard or use my examples that follow.) The ancient Greeks believed that the earth and the sky fell in love and all of Earth's creatures are the children of the earth. Long ago, the people of Norway and Sweden believed that the earth's creatures were pulled out of a boiling lake. And myths from Japanese and Indian cultures told of life being born from a huge egg.

The Bible is a book that is full of stories, too. But there is something very special about the Bible that makes it different than any other book in the world. *(Show the Bible and read directly from its pages; the translation here is the* New Living Translation.*)* Let me read to you from the New Testament book of 2 Timothy, chapter 3: "All Scripture is

inspired by God and is useful to teach us what is true and to make us realize what is wrong in our lives. It straightens us out and teaches us to do what is right" (v. 16 NLT). God used people to write down the words we find in the Bible, but the ideas and thoughts that are written down in these pages are inspired by God.

The Bible is God's word to us. God speaks to us through the Bible. It is not a book written just to be an interesting story or to teach us history. The Bible is a book written to change lives. God sent the scriptures to us so that we would know how much God loves us. The Bible tells us that Jesus came to take away our sins so that we would live forever with God. It's not a fairy tale, and it's not a myth. The Bible is the truest story that ever was. It is God's message of love to us. And God wants us to read the Bible and to listen to its words just as often as we can.

Dear God, thank you for giving us the Bible, which tells us the wonderful, true story of your love for us.

Notes

All Puffed Up

Preparation: For visual aids, bring along two noninflated balloons. Use a marker to draw a face on each balloon: a proud face for the Pharisee in the story (maybe with a turned up nose and a scowling mouth), and a humble face for the tax collector (eyes closed, small smile). To make it easier for children to blow up the balloons, blow them up ahead of time and then deflate them before the sermon.

I brought a couple of balloons this morning to help illustrate a story Jesus told—"The Pharisee and the Tax Collector." Jesus told this story to people who thought they were better than everyone else. These people belonged to a group of church leaders called Pharisees; these Pharisees looked down on anyone who was not just like them.

(Show balloons.) This balloon will play the part of the proud Pharisee, and this balloon will be the humble tax collector. I need two volunteers, one to hold each balloon. *(Hand "Pharisee" balloon to a child old enough to blow it up.)* Now as I read the story, whenever I look at the person holding the Pharisee balloon, I want you to blow some air into the balloon and then hold it shut. The person holding the tax collector balloon can just let it rest on your hand.

Jesus told this story: "Two men went to the Temple to pray. *[Look at Pharisee several times during the following—and allow time for the balloon to get larger and larger.]* One was a Pharisee, and the other was a dishonest tax collector. The proud Pharisee . . . prayed this prayer: 'I thank you, God, that

I am not a sinner like everyone else, especially like that tax collector! For I never cheat; I don't sin; I don't [think dirty thoughts], . . . and I give you a tenth of my income.' But the tax collector stood at a distance and dared not even lift his eyes to heaven as he prayed. Instead, he beat his chest in sorrow, saying, 'O God, be merciful to me, for I am a sinner'" (Luke 18:10-13 NLT).

Our Pharisee looks much different from the tax collector now. *(Let child hold up "Pharisee" balloon for all to see.)* The Pharisee is all puffed up with pride, but the tax collector is just laying there not daring to even look up. Do you know what Jesus said next? Jesus said that God was pleased with this sinner *(pick up limp balloon)* and not with the proud Pharisee. For the proud will be humbled *(pop or deflate "Pharisee" balloon)*, but the humble will be honored. *(Inflate the other balloon, tie it off, and let child take balloon with him or her.)* God raises up and honors those who admit they are sinners, but people who think they are better than others will be made humble.

Lord, we are sinners, but we know that you love us and forgive us. Thank you.

Notes

Zacchaeus

Preparation: Bring a beautiful and precious object, such as a necklace or pin or vase. Also bring a dirty paper bag and a fancy box or velvet bag.

This morning I have with me something very beautiful. *(Show children the object you brought.)* It's worth a lot to me. I like to show my [object] to other people so they can enjoy its beauty, too. Now I have to find something to keep it in. What do you think would be better, this dirty paper bag or this velvet bag? *(Show both containers. Let children answer.)* Something this beautiful should be kept in something that is clean and beautiful too, right? It just wouldn't be right if I placed the object I treasure into a dirty paper bag. *(Carefully place object into beautiful bag.)* But now, when I take this home to my room, I might notice that my room is too messy for this beautiful object, so I clean up my room. Then I notice that my room doesn't match the house, so I clean up the whole house. One beautiful and precious object can change and improve everything around it.

Today's Gospel story tells of a little, greedy, dishonest man who received something very precious, and his whole life changed because of it. Zacchaeus was a man who was disliked by everyone in town. He was a tax collector for the hated Roman government, and he often collected more money than he should have and kept it for himself.

When Jesus came to town, everyone went to see him and to listen to him teach. Zacchaeus went, too. But he was very short, and he couldn't see over the heads of the other people. He really wanted to see Jesus, so he climbed a tree.

Jesus walked right under that tree. And he stopped and looked up. And even though Jesus had never met Zacchaeus before, he called him by name. "Zacchaeus!" he said. "Quick, come down! For I must be a guest in your home today." At this point, I suppose that Zacchaeus nearly fell out of that tree with surprise. Something more valuable and precious than anything he had ever known had just walked into his life. Jesus, God's own Son, had invited himself to Zacchaeus's home. Jesus actually *cared* about Zacchaeus, even though everybody else seemed to hate him. Zacchaeus began to think about how he'd have to clean his house and get ready. Suddenly Zacchaeus knew that something else had to be cleaned. His dirty, shabby heart had to be made clean to receive the precious gift of Jesus' love. Right there, Zacchaeus repented of his dishonesty. He promised Jesus to make things right. His whole life changed because of Jesus' love.

Lord Jesus, come into our hearts, too, and help us get ready to greet you.

Notes

Life from Death

Preparation: Bring a growing plant to show and some seeds to pass out to the children.

The Gospel lesson for today talks about a group of people called Sadducees. Sadducees were Jews who believed that there was no life after death. Is that the same as what we believe? *(Let children answer.)* No. We know that God is preparing a place for us in heaven; and when we die, we go to be with Jesus.

It's easy to remember the Sadducees and what they believe, because their name describes how they must feel. It would be very sad to think that there is no life after death. So the Sadducees are very sad, you see—*Sadducee!*

Jesus told the Sadducees that God's children are raised up to new life when they die. When we reach the end of our life here on Earth, it may look like everything is over. But our life in heaven with Jesus is just beginning.

(Show plant and let children examine it as you describe it.) I brought a live plant with me this morning. It's green; it has leaves and roots. It is plain to us that the plant is alive. I also brought some seeds with me. *(Show seeds. Let children hold them.)* These seeds are hard and gray. I don't see any roots or leaves. These seeds look dead. What would happen if we had a funeral for them and buried them in the ground? *(Let children answer.)* They would start to grow, wouldn't they? We would soon see life springing from what we thought was dead.

It's the season of fall now. Plants are withering; leaves are falling. But even though the flowers and leaves are disappearing, we know what will happen come spring. The leaves will bud, and the flowers will return. In the same way, Christians know that death is not the end. We look forward to going to heaven to be with Jesus after we die. We aren't "sad, you see." We are happy because Jesus lives, and we look forward to living forever with Jesus.

Jesus, thank you for being with us now, and thank you for letting us live with you forever.

Notes

Dive to Safety

Preparation: Bring a toy submarine and a toy boat to help illustrate the sermon.

The Gospel lesson for today from Luke, chapter 21, is a little bit scary. Jesus is speaking about the end of the world, and he talks about things that will happen when that time comes. Jesus said that there will be earthquakes and wars and sickness all around. But Jesus tells his disciples that they don't need to be afraid: when the world comes to an end, the followers of God will be saved.

Reading these verses reminded me of a big storm. Imagine that you are on a boat way out in the ocean. *(Pantomime riding big waves with your toy boat.)* A mighty wind blows a huge storm in, and the winds start to tear at your sails and push your boat over. The waves get bigger and bigger until they tower like mountains all around you. The waves lift your boat up to the top of the wave, and then drop it down into the bottom. The skies light up with flashes of lightning, and thunder cracks right above your head. The rain is pouring down and blowing this way and that. It's a terrible storm!

If you were caught out in a storm like this, where could you go to be safe? Where could you quickly go to get away from the storm? *(Let children ponder the possibilities.)* Well, if you were in a submarine, you could dive down deep into the ocean. *(Demonstrate with the toy sub.)* If you dive beneath the surface of the ocean—even if it's only fifty feet or so below—the ocean is fairly calm and still. Even if a wild storm is raging on the surface, you can be calm and quiet below the surface.

All of us are going to have storms and rough waters. Life is not always easy. Sometimes bad things happen or we get hurt or we feel very, very sad. All of us have cried and been hurt before, and we will probably cry again. But our mighty God is like the deep part of the ocean. He is always right there beneath us and all around us. He is deep and calm and steady, and he doesn't change. When we hit rough waters in our lives, we can dive down into God's protection and comfort. We can pray and remember that God is holding us quietly and safely.

Deep and mighty God, thank you for being the calm beneath our storms. Help us to remember to turn to you for help and comfort when life gets rough. In Jesus name we pray. Amen

Notes

Eternal Kingdom

Preparation: Bring a chair and an elegant cloth to drape over it for a throne. If you would like, practice singing (or plan for a musical accompaniment) for the optional song at the end of this sermon.

Today is special. It is the last Sunday in the church calendar. Next week is the first Sunday in Advent, and that begins a new year in the church. This Sunday is also called "Christ the King Sunday."

What does a king do, and what does a king look like? *(Let children offer their responses.)* Kings sometimes wear crowns and sit on thrones. They make rules and watch over countries. There are still a few kings and queens in the world—the Queen of England and the King of Norway, for example. Could I have a volunteer come up and sit on the throne? *(Seat the volunteer on the "throne.")* You can be our ruler for awhile. Does a king or queen reign forever? Not at all. *(Replace ruler several times by letting other children take turns sitting on the "throne.")* There have been many, many kings and queens on this earth, and none of them sit on their thrones for very long. *(Remove last child from "throne.")*

Can anyone think of a king who rules forever? *(Let kids respond.)* Christ the King rules forever, doesn't he? His kingdom will have no end. Do you remember what Jesus was doing just a little while before he went back to his kingdom in heaven? He was doing something that we don't usually think kings do. Jesus was dying on a cross to save us from our sins.

There was a man hanging on another cross next to Jesus, and that man *really* had done things that were wrong. He knew that he deserved punishment, but he also knew that Jesus had done nothing wrong. And somehow he knew that Jesus was a king. As they were both hanging there dying, that man looked at Jesus and said, "Lord, remember me when you come into your kingdom." And Jesus looked at the man and said, "I tell you the truth; today you will be with me in Paradise." All of us are like that man hanging next to Jesus. We know that we've done many wrong things and deserve to be punished. But we also know that Jesus died in our place to save us. He is our King and Savior. And Jesus promises us, too, that we will always be with him in his kingdom.

(Optional) I have a simple song to teach you. It uses the words the man on the cross spoke to Jesus. Listen once and then sing along with me: "Jesus, remember me when you come into your kingdom. Jesus, remember me when you come into your kingdom." *(Invite children and, if you like, the entire congregation to sing along for three or four rounds.)*

Jesus, you are truly our King, and we thank you for giving us a kingdom that never ends.

Notes